Time Statues Revisited

Book One: On the Job

Robert F. Morgan

Copyright © 2023 Morgan Foundation Publishers

ISBN:
978-1-885679-17-8 (Paperback)
978-1-885679-25-3 (Ebook)

All rights reserved. No part of this book may be copied or reproduced, stored in a retrieval system, or transmitted in any form, or by any means mechanical, electronic, photocopying, recording or otherwise, without prior written permission of the publisher:

Morgan Foundation Publishers. Email:
morganfoundation@earthlink.net

Web page:
htpp://www.morganfoundationpublishers.com

Time Statues Revisited

Book One: On the Job

TABLE OF CONTENTS

Acknowledgements vii
Preview xi
Begin xiii

Introduction: Time Statues Revisited 1
ON THE JOB 11
Vaccine Suppositories: VS. 13
Saying Nothing 15
Inner Wisdom and Roberto Moulon 19
Cause and Effect 41
Crossover 43
Tinder Gold 47
Except For Your One Day 55
The Pattern's Suspect List 63
Targeted 69
The Primary Client 75
Max Returns: Ray's Next Life 87
An Honorary Catholic 119
A Mixed Method for Pattern Emergence (MMPE) 127
The Naked Latvian 137
Prisoners of War 147

Cleanliness in the Intensive Care Unit 157
Fire that Lasts. 159
Three Weddings 173
Alaskan Dream 183
Bonus. 187
Batacas. 189
Departures. 193
Ernst Beier, Ph.D. 197
Pat Norman. 203
Hans Toch, Ph.D. 207

References **211**
Robert F. Morgan. **217**
Other Books by Robert F. Morgan **219**

Acknowledgements

Thanks first to Asya Blue whose artistry and skills completed the 2021 Time Statues book and now this five book sequel series.

Otherwise, pretty much the same as in earlier work:

"I thank my past editors from different printing opportunities who encouraged me to write whatever I chose, even if without statistics, graphs, tables, footnotes, or scientific jargon. I was told to just call it *"Commentary"*. Or just write it.

In this I think of Valerie Hearn, with the staff at the *Cambridge University Press*, and Valentine McKay-Riddell, with the staff at the *Four Winds Journal* and the staff at the *Winds of Change Press*.

After decades of publishing about a hundred scientific journal articles and 14 books, it felt good to write freely and outside the confines of professional custom. I thank colleague Charles Tart who shared his own writing strategy: *'Just write what you really want to say. Then, as needed, you can add any citations, references, footnotes, and anything else an editor suggests.'*

Original material in this book is supplemented with my excerpts and illustrations from the *Four Winds Journal*, the Cambridge University Press *Journal of Tropical Psychology*, the *Bulletin of the International Association of Applied Psychology*: Supplement to *Applied Psychology*: *an International Review, Trauma Psychology in Context: International Vignettes and Applications from a Lifespan Clinical-Community Psychology Perspective, Opportunity's Shadow and the Bee Moth Effect: When Danger Transforms Community, Unfortunate Baby Names,* and the journal *International Psychology.*

Cited references are found at the end of the book in a consolidated reference section. As to the key mission of understanding the strange world we live in, and what we can do about it, I thank my Guides. Those include Robert Lee Green, Martin Luther King Jr., David Cheek, Michael Knowles, Rollo May, Nathan Hare, Fred Luskin, Sidney Farber, Robert Dattila, or mentors like Stanley Ratner, Bert Karon, Hans Toch, Lois Fisher, Helga Doblin, Cinnamon Morgan, Canadian-born Angel Morgan, plus the multitudes of my friends, teachers, parents and other relatives (my brother Nelson Morgan and forever sister Pat Norman come to mind). Also Michael Butz, Ron Slosky, Len Elkind, and the other thousands of students in six+ decades of teaching who have taught me much in return."

Now: For each of these five new volumes, I have special new appreciation for brilliant editor/inspiration Becky Owl Morgan, Guest contributor Bob Dattila, and the relentless motivating encouragement of Robert Lee Green, Carl Word, Tom Hanrahan, and Dorinda Fox. Roland Garcia impressively provided key focused feedback for a much improved reorganization. And Nelson Morgan's expertise.

Respect is due the earliest *Time Statues* reviewers that mixed insight and comment with their own encouragement: Lois Bridges, Robert Lee Green, Valentine McKay Riddell, Theodore Ransaw, Charles Tart, and Hans Toch. Great thanks also to Ben Tong for his many contributing illustrations along with insightful historical context.

Some material from my earlier books has been updated, modified, or excerpted here where it necessarily fits to join the original material. Sure, with author permission.

Octogenarian memory can be tricky. You may be curious about anybody deserving to be acknowledged here that I inadvertently left out. Hope not. But an option we can always use is the answers source we learn about all day long on TV commercials.

Ask your doctor.

Preview

"Getting it right"

Robert F. Morgan, San Francisco 2013

'WHAT DO YOU MEAN 'IT'S A BIT MUDDY'?'

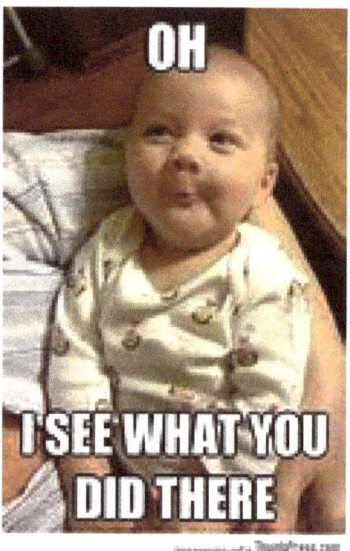

Begin

The Set

This is Book One of a five book set as follows:

Book One: *On the Job*

Book Two: *Language & Influence*

Book Three: *Citizenship*

Book Four: *Non-Human Relatives*

Book Five: *Human Family*

Optional Music Themes

Just below the chapter title is listed an optional theme, music or video. Some of readers may prefer to listen to this before, during, or after the reading of each chapter. If before, you can play it soundlessly in your mind while reading. You enjoy reading as a kind of movie experience with music enhancing the full experience. This feature is for you.

Other readers may find this a distraction.

The links may have changed since this printing; they may have been infiltrated by multiple commercials.

Or they may just want to avoid any online interference to their reading.

These readers may have grown up in the early or even pre-television generations where radio stories dominated. That required imagination to supply the picture and any music.

For them, we recommend skipping the optional themes entirely.

This omission is for them.

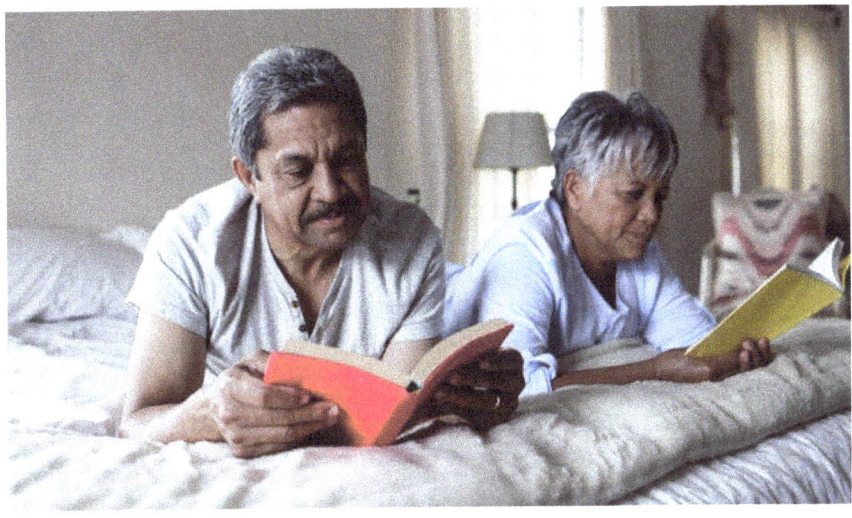

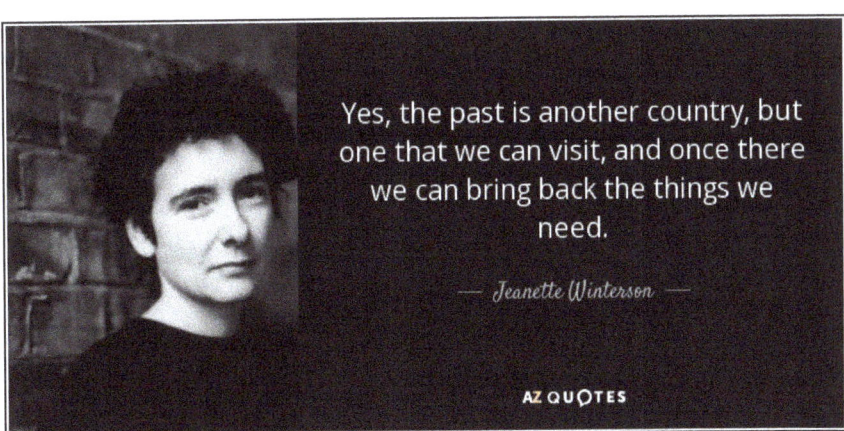

Introduction
Time Statues Revisited

Optional Theme: *Wizards* (Susan Anton) **https://www.youtube.com/watch?v=dyOTV8rqM9Q&ab_channel=NatashaDmitriyev**

Optional Theme: What Time Is It? (Ken Nordine) **https://www.youtube.com/watch?v=1_hdeT4BaRo&ab_channel=KenNordine-Topic**

> "When I was 5 years old, my mother always told me that happiness was the key to life. When I went to school, they asked me what I wanted to be when I grew up. I wrote down 'happy.' They told me I didn't understand the assignment, and I told them they didn't understand life."
>
> –John Lennon

> "Because we are born for a brief span of life, and because this spell of time that has been given to us rushes so swiftly and rapidly that with very few exceptions life ceases for the rest of us just when we are getting ready for it. It is not that we have a short time to live, but that we waste a lot of it. Our lifetime extends amply if you manage it properly."
>
> -Seneca, 65BCE, 2004 AD

Mammaries to Memories Revisited

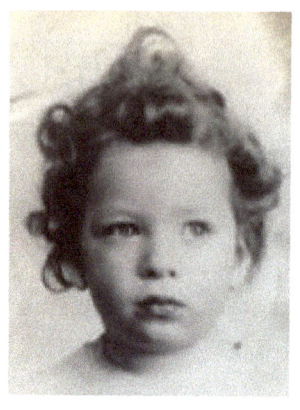

As a pre-school toddler, I already knew that I would grow up to be a writer. Everybody said I was a little Dickens.

Revisit: We were secure and warm, growing in safety. Growing so large that we began to be cramped. Here were the beginnings of desire for a larger apartment. Not to mention that the gentle rocking had become earthquakes.

In that moment or many moments later we first emerged into a new world. A mysterious world. Whirling shapes and colors, rumbling sounds. Made no sense.

We can explore though. Because we had the safety of the cord connecting us still to the warm safety we had left. Our air, our liquid energy. The lifeline is still there.

Hey! It got cut! Gone. Find a new way to breathe! We better figure out this weird place we are in. That's the primary mission. Fast as we can.

It takes a lifetime. And then only a *little* bit understood. Too late to go back to the womb. (On Mother's Day she will emphatically agree.)

The newborn learns to breathe the alien place's air. For energy it can suck nourishment from a giant's huge breast. This perspective might lead to a lifelong craving that will never be fully satisfied. Males seeking ever larger breasts? Females seeking to *have* ever larger breasts? Here for some could be a primal critical period leading to wealthier plastic surgeons and silicon merchants. (What about bottle-fed babies? Maybe alcohol drinks would sell better in baby bottle shaped containers?)

Not us. We moved on. We need not climb the beanstalk to get to the giant. We grew up and *became* the giant.

Whatever else we learned to do, our survival still depends on the mission. To understand this strange world. Remember what we learn. The important stuff.

Time is a place. Each moment is a statue in time, always rooted in that time and that place. Memory allows us to visit them.

After eight decades of this, I have amassed a library of memories. Stacks after stacks of time statues archives.

So much that it can take minutes or more to access just one memory and only with patience. Elders do better at this when we imagine our search as an ordering at a restaurant. Then, usually, it will come. Arriving late? But it will come.

From the viewpoint of age, we can view these memories in their entirety as a grand tapestry. Not necessarily arranged in order, chronologically.

What is a good guiding strategy for navigating these patterns, this treasure in an elder's experience? Maybe it's ones that were meaningful or fun. Sometimes both? Usually based on real past experience. Sometimes not. All of these can be shared.

Now: Well, at least some statues in time can be worth a visit. Or, on reflection, a revisit.

"Peter Rabbit" was a children's play I took my daughters to when they were very young. Peter began each day with great joy for the inevitable adventure. A day for him seemed like a whole season for us humans.

Remember in our own childhood how the beginning of the summer vacation seemed like the opening of endless days? For the shorter lifespan rabbit, each day was like that. It was a revelation for me. A fresh approach.

Jacob von Uexkull first made me aware more fully of the varying perceptual time world of animals:

"Karl Ernst von Baer has made it clear that time is the product of a subject. Time as a succession of moments varies from one Umwelt to another, according to the number of moments experienced by different subjects within the same span of time. A moment is the smallest indivisible time vessel, for it is the expressions of an indivisible elementary sensation, the so-called moment sign. As already stated, the duration of a human moment amounts to 1/18 of a second. Furthermore, the moment is identical for all sense modalities, since all sensations are accompanied by the same moment sign.

The human ear does not discriminate eighteen air vibrations in one second, but hears them as one sound. It has been found that eighteen taps applied to the skin within one second are felt as even pressure.

Cinematography projects environmental motions onto a screen at their accustomed tempo. The single pictures then follow each other in tiny jerks of 1/18 second.

If we wish to observe motions too swift for the human eye, we resort to slow-motion photography. This is a technique by which more than eighteen pictures are taken per second, and then projected at a normal tempo. Motor processes are thus extended over a longer span of time, and processes too swift for our human time-tempo (of 18 per second), such as the wing beat of birds and insects, can be made visible. As slow motion-motion photography slows motor processes down, the time contractor speeds them up. If a process is photographed once an hour and then presented at the rate of 1/18 second, it is condensed into a short space of time. In this way, processes too slow for our human tempo, such as the blossoming of a flower, can be brought within the range of our perception.

The question arises whether there are animals whose perceptual time consists of shorter or longer moments than ours, and in whose Umwelt motor processes are consequently enacted more slowly or more quickly than in ours.

The first experiments of this kind were made by a young German scientist. Later, with the collaboration of another, he studied especially the reaction of the fighting fish to its own mirror image. The fighting fish does not recognize its own reflection if is shown him eighteen times per second. It must be presented to the fighting fish at least thirty times per second. A third student trained the fighting fish to snap toward their food if a gray disc was rotated behind it. On the other hand, if a disc with black and white sectors was turned slowly, it acted as a "warning sign," for in this case the fish received a light shock when they approached their food. After this training, if the rotation speed of the black and white disc was gradually increased, the avoiding reactions became more uncertain at a certain speed, and soon thereafter they shifted to the opposite. This did not happen until the black sectors followed each other within 1/50 second. At this speed the black and white signal had become gray. This proves conclusively that in the world of these fish, who feed on fast moving prey, all motor processes – as in the case of slow-motion photography – appear at reduced speed.

A vineyard snail is placed on a rubber ball which, carried by water, slides under it without friction. The snail's shell is held in place by a bracket. Thus the snail, unhampered by its crawling movements, remains in the same place. If a small stick is then moved up to its foot, the snail will climb up on it. If the snail is given one to three taps with the stick each second, it will turn away, but if four or more taps are administered per second, it will begin to climb onto the stick. In the snail's world a rod that oscillates four times per second has become stationary. We may infer from this that the snail's receptor time moves at a tempo of three to four moments per second. As a result, all motor processes in the snail's world occur much faster than in ours. Nor do its own motions seem slower to the snail than ours do to us." (von Uexkull 1957, Morgan 2005)

Even within our human species great individual variations of time perception exist.

Working with older people, I often saw anxiety about how few years of life it seemed that they had left. I had been working with the full spectrum of human aging and life extension experts, Jim Birren to Timothy Leary. They approached the subject with biology as cause and with psychology as consequence.

What if we reversed the order? What if seniors with the life expectancy of less than a decade approached each day as a season in itself? Instead of ten birthdays and out, why not 3,650 individual seasons to savor, one at a time?

To do this, the senior would need to slow the rocketing passage of time engendered by similar days. Magnified by retirement or illness, one day is much like another. They go by in a flash. This may be comforting but life then goes by quickly. But if each day was differentiated as its own adventure, time will slow down. Life extension occurs experientially. For some, those who accomplished this, they said it helped very much.

We're not rabbits. We live much longer. Or so we can learn to do.

Can each of our days and the moments within them become simply statues of adventure in time?

Building on the first *"Time Statues"* book from 2021, once again we come to Einstein and Vonnegut: the temporal community is a place. Each day we finish is fixed for all time. Or is it? We can revisit, this time for new and more challenging ones.

This time we go to the even more interesting ones, although many are protected by metaphorical police tape. Worth the trip? (To help, each chapter begins with a link to a musical theme.)

As we get older, of what we usually regret, it is more often what we did not do than what we did. Either way, a revisit to worthwhile remote events seems worth the return trip. Despite some statues best forgotten.

To navigate effectively in our own normal environment, it is entirely reasonable to consider time as linear and irreversible.

A nonlinear approach will naturally unearth exceptions. The passage through time carries us forward, evolving and adapting. In our nonlinear world, if we are open to it, we can find ways to detour against the current as part of our healthy development. It makes for a richer tapestry than had been expected.

Each moment we live includes our action as our art. Good art or bad art, all that we do sculpts a second-by-second statue to inhabit that time and that place.

The artist continues to live in the limited moments of this lifespan community. Yet the consequences of this art can travel ever further, transcending dangers and obstacles, to shape a better future for our human community.

In this way, we can too.

Star Fleet on a shopping spree.

Time Tip: On the first day of each month, doctors often drop finished patients from their lists. These revisions make that day the very best day to schedule appointments where any other time may be a wait of months. Time pattern awareness can be practical.

ON THE JOB

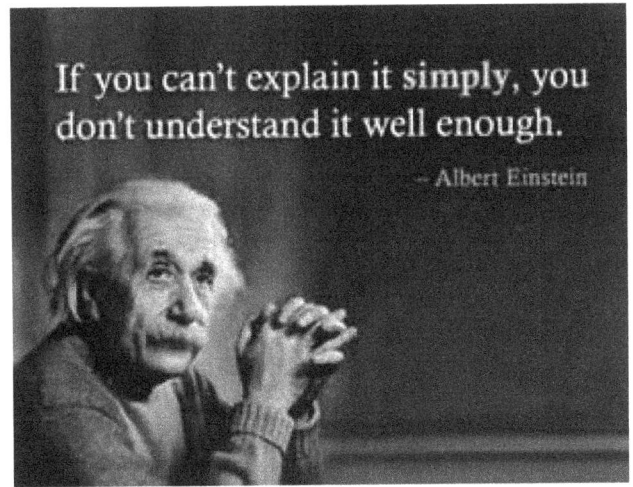

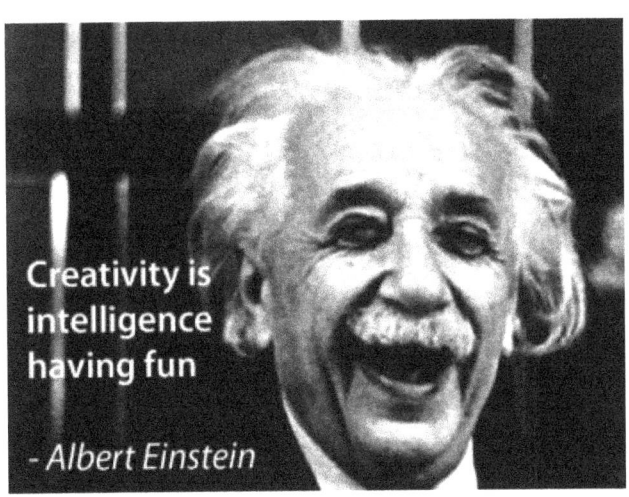

A *New* Booster Distribution Model

Optional Theme: *Here Comes the Sun* (G. Harrison) **https://www.youtube.com/watch?v=H3OhtUtqY7Q&ab_channel=I%C5%9F%C4%B1lKaya)**

Vaccine Suppositories: VS

Skip those needles in your shoulder.
Time release is an end in itself.

Caution: Only one to a customer.
No repeats. VS will fit you where the good Lord split you.

(VS might be mass produced in Elephant Butte NM USA. Or might not.)

Saying Nothing

Optional Theme: *While My Guitar Gently Weeps (Santana, Yo Yo Ma, India Arie)* **https://www.youtube.com/watch?v=GXW5MY-tif8&ab_channel=AVaffair7Multi-Genre-Multi-Generational**

Dr. Leonard Miller, Leon, was a psychiatrist at San Francisco's Center for Special Problems (CSP). He wasn't viewed as belonging to the group of psychiatrists working there. Instead he was a member of the group of individuals that belonged to no group (mathematicians' paradox).

Not particularly friendly, this elder man with the trim goatee radiated individuality. That was exemplified by his staunch refusal to ever prescribe medications. His prescription pad might otherwise contain a behavioral prescription (*"Buy her flowers and apologize"*) or important notes to himself (*"Fishing with grandson this Saturday: Bring treats"*).

Staff usually just left Leon alone. So naturally we became friends.

I slouched past his office one morning, feeling the weight of my five part time jobs and the struggles of the people there I was trying to help, plus my own. Leon yelled: *"Hey Atlas! Put the earth down and rest for a while."*

Strange maybe. But that memory always helped me do just that. Sometimes there *is* a perfect thing to say.

In the 1970s the city was over-loaded with special problems, known also as unique individuals. CSP staff were often regarded in more traditional mental health centers as special problems in their own right- creative, effective, famous, and very hard to categorize.

Still, CSP took on clients the regular centers preferred not to see, even in San Francisco: addicts, sexual life style pioneers, and even much sought felons. And while the five other county centers left their empty offices to do community outreach, the CSP was the one that still gave face-to-face psychotherapy to the city's citizens.

Leon's reputation rested more than anything else on his evening contact groups with self-selected suicidal walk-ins. A contact group was a gathering of people without cost, record, or paper. In fact, CSP was proud to be the last such center in the country to give clients the option to be un-digitized.

(CSP Director Gene Turrell, formerly with Kinsey's group, specialized in transforming felons wanted by the law, including killers, with the belief that by doing so in absolute confidence he was saving more victims. Without that, they naturally would not come in. When law officers sat in his office demanding information on any of these, Gene, a chain smoker, would shut his office door and then fill the room with smoke. Gene looked like 'Lurch' from the Addams family, wore size 18 shoes.

The law would retreat without what they came for, smoke blown up their visit.

Leon let me sit in one night with his contact group. One of the 13 people there said: *"I have nothing to live for!"* Leon: *"Yes! That's your reason."* Some were confused, other contact group regulars smiled. Leon went on to explain that finding your individual purpose in existing on this earth was the most important thing you can do. *"Start looking"* he said. Then others reported their progress.

Yes, Leon was very existential in his approach. It worked.

Our staff gathering place was Ernie's, a Chinese restaurant a block from work on Polk Street. One day I walked in to see something I had never seen before. Leon sat quietly alone in a corner table with tears streaming down his cheeks. A waitress we knew whispered: *"His grandson had an accident at school and died yesterday. Very sad."* Leon's grandson was the happiest part of his days. Whenever he spoke of him, he would transform into smiles. Clearly, his grandson was Leon's purpose in living.

And now I sat next to Leon. He acknowledged me with a nod but said nothing. Whatever could I say to this good man that would help him through this trauma? I could think of nothing. So I just put my hand on his forearm and sat with him in silence.

Leon eventually pushed his untouched plate of food away and quietly said *"Thank you Atlas. I appreciated that."*

He left the restaurant and wasn't seen at work for a few weeks.

When he returned, his contact groups re-commenced. Leon seemed to have found there another purpose for his existence.

And I had learned this:

When you can think of nothing helpful to say, nothing is what to say.

Inner Wisdom and Roberto Moulon

Optional Theme: *Magic Man* (Heart)
https://www.youtube.com/watch?v=3vlAdMeZSfw&ab_channel=SuperKevinheart

In 1966, Roberto Moulon was the psychiatrist in charge of Hawaii's hospitalized patients from the Neighbor Islands (outside Oahu).

His family ethnicity was French Guatemalan Indian. He looked somewhat like a tanned older Herve Villechaize from TV's *Fantasy Island*.

I was a psychologist working with Hawaii State Hospital's Metropolitan Honolulu patients. My psychologist colleagues were following an Existentialist practice, which was great. But Moulon had a Freudian perspective and that was worth a listen as well. Plus tales of his past private practice. A sample follows.

Inner Wisdom

Dr. Moulon told me about a new patient in his past private practice. A large anxious man inhabited his couch while Roberto sat behind the young man's view in Freudian traditional pose, casually lighting his pipe. The patient rambled on for some time but finally got to the fear that had brought him to this psychiatrist. He said he had been unable to have an erection during a sexual opportunity with a woman he had met in Rome. He wondered if this meant he was damaged or getting old before his time. Moulon, in a quiet but authoritative French accent from behind the patient, told him to say more about the specific event.

With this invitation, the young man went on: *"We were somewhat drunk but still able to walk. The night was beautiful. People were everywhere enjoying their time together. We came to a huge fountain by the Vatican. Reminded me of the movie La Dolce Vita."*

The Trevi Fountain, Rome.

He continued: *"In that very moment it WAS a sweet life for us! We were spontaneous. Ignoring the other people around us, we stripped off our clothes and jumped into the water around the fountain. Let the water fall over us. We kissed. She pressed against me. I have always risen to such occasions. But not this time. My penis refused to rise. Doctor PLEASE! Tell me what this means!"*

Moulon was silent for a moment while he puffed on his pipe. Finally his authoritative voice intoned: *"The meaning? Well of course. Clearly your penis has more sense than you do."*

Not the Trevi Fountain, Rome. They love to frolic in water too though.

The Psychiatrists

At our hospital, psychiatrists fell into two categories. To begin with, all had been trained as medical doctors before moving into their psychiatric specialty. Most of them in that training, usually a residency, never had any supervised experience doing psychotherapy. Instead they learned the biomedical tools of prescribing psychiatric medications, the sadly destructive electroconvulsive treatment (ECT), and, in those days, even lobotomies (still recommended then by our hospital administrator). These methods were at best unhelpful and at worst destructive, occasionally lethal. This left most psychiatrists in the first non-psychotherapy category at a loss to be effective with the hospital patients. Further, some of these doctors were all but hopeless at working anywhere else.

An immigrant physician from Turkey comes to mind as an example. He spoke no English at all so he could not understand any of his patients or staff. Diverse as Hawaii was, nobody on hospital staff knew Turkish so as to be his translator. He lasted in his job for quite a few months though.

In category two, on the other hand, a few of the physicians had excellent psychotherapy training. Of these our Roberto Moulon was the most experienced and probably the most *akamai* or wisest of his psychiatrist peers.

The state of Hawaii released an employee sick leave study for the previous calendar year, broken down for our hospital by discipline. The psychologists and social workers had accumulated *zero* days of sick leave in that time. We pretty much never felt we could take any sick leave to miss a work day, given the substantial immediate need in our wards. The nurses and psychiatrists had the most sick leave days, higher than the state employee average for their discipline. In addition, they both had the largest turnovers. Other studies found psychiatry to have excessive suicide and drug addiction issues.

We understood the nursing statistics. As a group, they earned the least of any hospital disciplines while expected to do the most work, often with long extra hours. Compared to their psychiatrist supervisors, they did more for less. Much more for much less. The nurses also fell into two categories. The beginning nurses were usually highly motivated to learn, dedicated to their patients, and expected success in their chosen career. They knew they had a challenging job. Certainly they could have gone into a less stressful nursing environment. For them it was a career they cared about. They were also very decent people. Over the years, a few of them survived to be highly effective long term senior nurses. But others burned out or became cynical, expecting little success at work and less reward for their effort. No wonder their absences total and turnover were high.

The psychiatrists without the training they needed to do their job well were naturally stressed and it showed in the statistics. Worse, they were the ones chosen to lead the hospital supervision and administration, again requiring people skills few of them had available. They could feel frustrated, stressed, unappreciated. Even when by some luck they did manage success at the magic they felt was required of them, anticipated staff or patient applause was lacking.

'WHAT DO YOU MEAN 'IT'S A BIT MUDDY'?'

Of course, many were only there to qualify for licensing to do private practice and would leave as soon as they had acquired the needed hours. Some though, lacking the talent they needed, still gave it their best. This could lead to legend. Here are two examples:

(1) Love in Hawaii

"A psychiatrist claimed to cure locked ward patients at the state hospital from a distance. He sits in his office with their files, never meeting them, and practices existential extremism: he assumes their traumatic pathology stems from him, apologizes, and wishes them love. He reports that his patients get better while the rest get worse. This got a lot of play in the media. Well, if this marvelous effect can be validated, it could mean more than a psychiatrist finding ways to avoid patients and collect a paycheck, interesting in its own right.

It would assume a certain existential narcissism: he is the cause and cure of the trauma of others. Of course, it might also be that the normal treatment of psychiatric patients in a locked ward is iatrogenic and that by withholding treatment (no ECT or psychiatric drugs or interpersonal intervention) and staying in his office he is demonstrating placebo power, moral treatment, or just leaving people alone (Morgan, 2005b). On the other hand, if all the current problems of our human community truly come from him, he needs to start apologizing and sending global love without delay." (Morgan, 2012)

(2) Dining on Air

Another psychiatrist at Hawaii State Hospital, before my time there, completed a legendary experiment. He had tried fasting, vegan diets, and other cultural paths to enlightenment. By reaching a higher plain of his own existence, he had confidence he could be more effective with his patients.

By general staff observation, he lacked the ability to benefit any of his patients. Despite this, all agreed that he at least had the will to do so.

The gap between psychiatric training and successful treatment fit was a common stress for hospital physicians with a conscience. This man was one such.

And so it was that they tried not to be appalled when one Monday morning the psychiatrist announced that he had not eaten or had anything to drink all week end.

The one exception, he had read of and practiced nourishment only from the air itself. He was now a *"Breatharian"*.

While those practicing this technique still imbibe liquids, their psychiatrist followed the strictest path he had found, one in search of the best outcome, quickly. He would dine only on air and sunlight.

His nursing staff was dubious but also relieved he was doing this first on himself before prescribing it for his patients. Or worse, for them.

The psychiatrist managed almost a full day of work before he was carried out on a stretcher. He was said to have survived but never returned to his hospital job.

The staff wondered who or what would take his place next.

Note: I am reminded of my stay once at a profoundly underfunded program's weekly report to the full faculty of the overall for-profit university, with most of the student tuition going to the owning corporation.

I told them of the farmer who had run short of feed for his horse and fed the animal only the half ration left. To the farmer's surprise, the horse adjusted to this meager meal in a few days and worked as before. The joyful farmer called a meeting to share his finding with all the other farmers. In preparation he cut the horse's rations in half again. It took longer for the horse to adjust but that he did. When the meeting finally convened, the horse's owner shared this opportunity to save on feed with enthusiasm, despite the ending of his talk when he breathlessly announced that only days before he had cut his horses daily ration to zero. Just when he was ready to announce his success to all of them, he had some bad fortune. The horse had unexpectedly died.

Following this unusual report of my own, the top administrator present stood and said *"Dr. Morgan, please elevate that sad story you just told us with at least something more positive!"*

I did my best: *"Here in my program we like to think of our resources as being like a glass 5% full."*

Candid honesty means always having your bags packed.

Tom Thumb

A brilliant colleague from those days in Hawaii, Albuquerque psychologist Joe Alexander, emailed me a reminder of his experience with Dr. Moulon: *"Roberto was our moderator for our afternoon monthly case review. Psychiatrists, Psychologists, interested Social Workers (only LaVey Lau actually) took turns presenting clinical cases. Then Roberto would make observations. We took turns presenting and taking minutes. Sometimes the psychiatric residents and psychology interns were invited. My favorite session was a presentation by Moulon called 'Seven Sick and Sinful Sisters'. "*

Yes. Comparing Roberto to most of the other psychiatrists was a low bar. Moulon was really great at his work. Or calling.

I didn't get to hear Joe's favorite *"Seven Sick and Sinful Sisters"* but I can share my most memorable case conference with Roberto. About a deadly Tom Thumb.

These headlines were remarkably bad and all over the state. A chronic mental patient, recently returned to her family on a conditional discharge, had murdered all five of her children, including a baby.

She was eventually sent to the care of a locked hospital ward run by Dr. Moulon.

Nobody on his staff wanted anything to do with this patient. All refused to treat her.

Hawaii in that era put child care above all other priorities, probably still does. A killer of children, especially her own, was the worst human being they could imagine. Hate for any patient was rare in this professional group. This one they hated.

Moulon had a staff rebellion on his hands.

He called a case conference meeting for the very next morning. Invited me to join him there. Which in Hawaii was at 7 AM (so the day could end early enough for daylight swimming and surfing). I avoid mornings but in this case I definitely agreed. I thought Roberto would need some support.

He did not.

Once assembled around the conference table, we all turned to Moulon at its head. He sat there elevated on his chair, and quietly asked for a brief status report on the new patient. A nurse complied.

The patient was heavily sedated and slept in a locked room. In her waking moments she denied doing anything wrong, asked about her children, she dropped back to sleep. Her body functions and diet were normal. She was more than in denial. She was delusional, psychotic. No adequate reality contact. Hopeless?

Then a social worker briefly reiterated what everybody in the state already knew. The patient had been in and out of the state hospital for years. In each of five of her exits she had become pregnant. Her children, including the baby, had been in foster care but had been reassembled to be with her for this last discharge. The hospital administrator, a psychiatrist, had personally approved this arrangement, saying that children belonged with their mother. The administrator was now providing no comment other than saying it was in Dr. Moulon's hands.

(We all knew that the administrator had also released another patient as cured who subsequently climbed a tower and shot people to death. The administrator, affirming her decision that this now deceased killer was mentally healthy at discharge, had blamed it on an overseen minor brain tumor found in the autopsy. Though medical research has yet to find a part of the brain capable of directing somebody to climb a tower and shoot people. Now, with this new patient, she was fully hands off. It was Moulon's headache.)

When all the reports were done, tensely and tersely, Roberto let them settle for a minute. Until finally we had all turned to him for comment, direction. Tense crowd.

Finally he calmly said *"I will tell you a story. You may not understand it. I will have no interruptions. When I am done, we may discuss the relevance."* He continued.

The calm voice with the French accent from this brilliant man in that early morning seemed unworldly. Especially as he began. But we all listened.

"You surely recall the story of little Tom Thumb. He and his brothers, also little, had left home and were far from anywhere they knew. Why

they left home did not matter at the time because it was getting dark and they were hungry. Wait! They smelled some delicious food. It was coming from a very big cabin on a hill. Quickly Tom led them to the cabin door, much taller than they had ever seen, and Tom knocked on it hard with his walking stick.

The door soon opened and a giant woman looked down at them.

Tom asked if they could come in. The night was dark now and they were hungry.

The giant considered, smiled, and invited them in, just in time for supper.

Tom and his brothers sat down at a huge table. There already were the giant's children. They were the same in number as those with Tom although, being giant's children, they must have been much younger since they were all about the same height as Tom. The giant mother sat at one end of the table and the giant father at the other. The food already prepared was delicious and everybody ate until full, maybe a little more than that.

The giant mother promised an even better breakfast and then led all the children to a bedroom so they could sleep after such a meal. She left them alone and shut the door.

The bedroom needed no beds as the floor was as soft as a fine mattress. The giant's children had seemed shy to Tom at first but even now they spoke not at all to their guests. Soon all were asleep, the giant woman's children on one side while Tom and his brothers soon were asleep on the other.

Tom woke in the middle of the night. Maybe he first just wanted to answer a call of nature. He opened the bedroom door and could hear some noise from the kitchen. Looking for directions, he walked to the kitchen door. Here stood the giant mother talking to her giant husband who was seated at the table, back to Tom. The mother was sharpening a huge knife and a massive pot of boiling water was over the fire.

Tom heard her say to her husband "Almost time to slice off their heads and pop them in the pot. They'll be a great stew for breakfast."

The giant husband said "Now? But it's dark in there. No moon tonight. How will you know which ones to slice?"

His wife said "All our guests have goofy stocking hats and they went to bed with them on. Our children don't sleep with any hats. Could do it with my eyes shut."

"You'll have to. Its pitch dark in there."

At this, Tom ran back to the bedroom, He took off his hat and the hats of his brothers, putting each one on the head of one of the giant's children. His eyes were adapted to the crack of light coming through the bedroom door from the kitchen. Then he very quietly woke his brothers, shushed them, and all slipped out of the cabin. Just as they left, Tom looked back through a window and saw the giant mother with her huge knife and a massive bag enter the bedroom. Breakfast will be a surprise for sure.

Then Tom and his hatless brothers ran until they were safe."

Moulon stopped there. Paused. Then: "*As to our new patient. What do you think she thought she was doing when she killed her own children?*"

And then he told us.

Moulon had been working with the patient herself during her lucid moments. At first she denied everything, even insisting they were all alive and fine. She said it was all a misunderstanding. She had just killed mice on her lawn, not people. Mice? Maybe roaches or rats? Not clear she said.

A neighbor had reported to police that the patient had just backed her car out of the driveway on a sunny afternoon. Her children were playing on the lawn near the driveway. Except for the baby who had crawled under a rear tire. The neighbor saw the woman driver get out of the car to see what all the yelling was about. Then she saw what was left of the baby after the car tire had crushed it. The children on the lawn were crying and screaming. The neighbor went home and called the police. When the police got there, all the children had been killed and their mother was unconscious. Comatose. Overwhelmed.

Killing her baby was a genuine accident. The rest were a hopeless delusional exit from an impossible situation. She was the giant mother who had killed her own children without meaning to. Tom Thumb was fictitious. Her overwhelming tragedy was not. The dead children could no longer be helped. If she could be helped, even a little, we should try.

Moulon said he would assign himself to continue treatment. Then he assigned all of us to either be kind with any contact or to avoid all contact if we had no kindness in us.

We filed away quietly. The rebellion was over. Sadness not.

Over the next few weeks Moulon called on every bit of his brilliance to build a relationship with this lost woman. He made progress. She was his primary client. Not us. Not the administrator. Not the press. Not the public. He did his best and it helped.

He warned me that her delusion was clearly a functional protection against acknowledging the horror of her murder of her own children. When she lifts that delusional protection, she becomes vulnerable. That would be the most dangerous time for her. He planned to guide her through it.

On a Friday he told me, elated, she had dropped her delusion. She was heavily sedated again. Moulon prepared for the key therapy on the following Monday.

We wondered together what in life could a person do, coming to grips with what she had done. Maybe spend the rest of her life volunteering at the Kalaupappa Leper Colony? Study law in a cell? Develop spirituality?

Clearly it would be her choice and only after some serious incarceration could she make such a decision. That was Friday

On Sundays a minister, claiming to be the patient's minister, had visited. He was not her minister. In fact she had no such person in her life. This "minister" was there to get her to admit her crime. On that last Sunday visit she did so. He told her she would roast in hell and everybody would always hate her. She didn't deserve to live! Not worth any more care or the therapy Moulon had planned.

The staff escorted the fake minister out when they heard him yelling these things at the patient.

That night they found she had hung herself in her locked room.

Monday morning was possibly Moulon's worst day. Not great for any of us, but especially crushing for Roberto. What to do with such grief?

Only one thing to do. We took on the next case. One we both had patients involved in.

And we learned something new.

Sibling Bondage: A Parricide and his Brother

Roberto Moulon and I coined the term "sibling bondage" as a pathological opposite to the better known and frequently manifested "sibling rivalry".

An example follows from my 2012 *"Trauma Psychology in Context"* book.

"The Discovery of Sibling Bondage: A Parricide & his Brother

The second Manuel killed his father, he was able to love him again. But now his anger was satisfied, he had a larger problem. Putting down the shotgun, he called the police and said **"I kill my father. Come get me."**

Then he said nothing more: not when they came, not in jail, and not when he was carried off the plane frozen to his chair en route to Hawaii State Hospital. He took up residence in his catatonic state and remained in apparent safety there for the duration.

Only days after his arrival, his younger brother Anthony was also flown in for hospitalization.

Anthony was the youngest, a stocky teenager, and, far from catatonic, was swearing vengeance to his father's ghost, or so he said. Mother, the sole survivor in the family home, had decided Anthony needed to be flown to Oahu to be with his brother and away from her. She was considered to be mentally disabled but she wasn't stupid. Speaking to invisible beings, after Manuel's action, just didn't seem right.

Anthony was assigned to my Young Adult Day Program while Manuel was taken under the care of Dr. Roberto Moulon. Aa psychoanalyst formerly of the Menninger Clinic, he began coordinating the treatment of the brothers with me. This was not always easy.

Anthony was quite friendly and rational with two exceptions. The first was whenever he saw Dr. Moulon, who resembled his deceased father. At this time, he would bellow and chase the psychiatrist into his office. Moulon found it difficult to relate effectively with Anthony from the safe side of his locked office door.

The second stressor was the monthly visit of his mother. On viewing her, Anthony would punch the air and loudly swear vengeance for his dead father. Soon Mother was only visiting Manuel, even though these visits were somewhat unusual: Manuel sat frozen in his chair where he had been carried outside to the front grass and sunshine. For hours Mother would sit quietly next to him along with some local relatives. Not a word was ever said beyond **"Hello Manuel"** *and* **"Goodbye Manuel".**

Moulon and I sifted through the family history.

Manuel and Anthony were the youngest of a large Portuguese family on a small rural island. Their mother was barely functional, her great achievement being the household cooking and cleaning.

Her husband was an absolute tyrant, completely controlling all under his roof with regular beatings. He alone would go into town and shop. His children were discouraged from going to school and were not allowed to speak unless spoken to first by him. The expression 'poor communication' does little justice to the managed silences under this father's regime. The children left home as soon as they could: boys joined the army while girls got pregnant and married. Eventually only Manuel and Anthony remained.

Of these, Manuel was his father's favorite. They worked together in the fields in rare and quiet harmony.

Anthony, at 15 the youngest, was another story. Although he was as large as Manuel, he had a heart murmur. Mother kept him close. So close in fact, he slept with her right up to the day he was hospitalized. Father wanted Anthony to work in the fields with his brother but, apparently for the first time in their marriage, she refused, saying she would leave if Anthony had to do such work. The Patriarch possibly did not see himself doing cooking or cleaning. He gave in.

Anthony went to public school and did reasonably well. This favoritism was not missed by Manuel. One day Manuel himself ordered his brother to come out to the fields and work. Anthony declined and their parents supported him.

The next day Manuel went into town to enlist in the Army. Unfortunately for him, the recruiters were now required to give an intelligence test which he failed, nor did it occur to him to apply for officer training instead.

Manuel returned home in a foul mood. He once again worked with his father in the fields but began muttering that his father was a communist and a "revisionist", words heard on the family radio.

It may well be that taking Anthony's side was a revisionist thing for his father to do, given Manuel's former status as his father's favored child. The father did not know what a revisionist was but he knew that a 'communist' was supposed to be something very bad. He finally beat Manuel until he fell into the fields, covered with blood and bruises.

That night Manuel borrowed his father's shotgun and killed him in his sleep.

*As time went by, Moulon's work with Manuel paid off. Manuel began moving again and in a few weeks he was one of the happiest residents in the hospital. He worked hard at his **'industrial therapy'** (which meant hospital garbage collection) and developed a close bond with Doctor Moulon, his therapist and father figure. ("But I'll never take him on a hunting trip" said Moulon.).*

Anthony for his part thrived in my Young Adult Program. Despite his harsh background, he was of normal intelligence and made many new friends.

Oh he still chased Roberto Moulon into his office (but now smiled when he did so) and became quietly anxious when Mother visited. But that was all.

He also spent time with his brother and often left him gifts.

*Asked about Anthony, Manuel would smile and say "**My brother loves me now.**"*

*Asked about Manuel, Anthony would say "**He killed him for me.**"*

Why had Anthony been so belligerent at home, hallucinating a dead parent?

Moulon believed it was guilt for wishing his father dead. This may be but certainly there was trauma involved.

Eventually, Anthony explained it to me. He believed in an afterlife in which his father's malevolent ghost was still around. Only this ghost was worse than his father had been before: Father was now invisible and with ghostly powers, Father could tell that Anthony wanted him dead more than Manuel did. Father would hurt him if he didn't swear vengeance and be convincing. On the plus side, Anthony believed that his father's ghost could only be found in his old house or by his mother's side. So he enjoyed his new life on Oahu without trauma.

And why chase Dr. Moulon?

"At first I didn't like the way he looked"

"Like your Father"

"Yes."

"Now you know he's not your father."

"Oh yes. But now I like the way he runs."

And Anthony smiled.

The children of loving and competent parents normally experience a rivalry for parental affection. This **"sibling rivalry"** *is quite normal. On the other hand, children of abusive or non-competent parents may band together against the common enemy but this is a relationship based on trauma and danger. As such, it can be handicapping or even violently destructive. Moulon and I decided to call this* **"sibling bondage"** *(Moulon & Morgan, 1967).*

If our perspective was correct, then the older siblings would soon also be in distress. Checking with the local clinic on the Mother's island, within weeks of the death of their father, every one of the brothers and sisters had been in for treatment. The eldest daughter had recurring nightmares of an open coffin in her living room into which she dared not look.

Under Moulon's consultation, all received therapist encouragement to accept their anger and its Shadow, a death wish for their Father, as a normal traumatic reaction to his brutality, and to face his memory without guilt or fear.

Today, I would add forgiveness as well, but in this instance Moulon's directions were effective. Shadows lose their power when a light is shined on them. All the brothers and sisters recovered.

A community can also be led into sibling bondage, transformed by trauma, members bound together into a closed system by hatred.

This bond is also pathological and needs healing."

*   *   *

That was then. How about now?

In looking at our contemporary world, we can see sibling bondage play out on a much broader political and social stage.

Cultish domestic terrorism is such an extreme.

Or even the lesser taking of horse de-wormer while shunning life-saving vaccines.

Which body part should be credited with more sense?

What would Dr. Moulon say if he were here to observe?

We sure miss him.

Cause and Effect

Optional Theme: *Basted in Blood* (SNL) http://vimeo.com/54035320

The busiest day of the year for plumbers is the day after Thanksgiving.

Or, depending, on any other family celebration day.

Protocol Note: *After all have eaten and the time has come to clear the table, do NOT refer to the leftover food as "the remains".*

Crossover

Optional Theme: *Firebird* (YouTube Orchestra 2011) <u>https://www.youtube.com/watch?v=kd1xYKGnOEw&ab_channel=YouTubeSymphonyOrchestra2011</u>

Greenville burned to the ground not long ago.

Before, it had been a small town in the majestic Maidu Indian Country of northern California's mountains, just miles below the Lake Almanor reservoir. Here as it was:

The closest city was a two hour drive to Reno. Other American Indian tribes were present here and there, plus some white self-styled *"Outlaw"* bands that descended occasionally to pillage the *"flat-landers"* in Chico.

Back in the late 1990s a small clinic was established for the underserved people of Greenville. I was the only psychologist in that half of the county, so it kept me busy.

J was one of my patients. A white woman in her 40s, originally born in Wisconsin, she had lived her adult life there in Greenville with her husband, a pet household pig, and friendly neighbors.

Everybody liked J. I was no exception. She was the first to share with me the expression that her spouse *"always gets his panties in a bunch"*.

She carefully described her home wood stove as consisting of just three basic parts: *"Lifter, Leg, and Poker"*, followed by an endearing laugh.

Her problems were resolvable much as her visits were enjoyable. My wife gladly drove her past the Greenville known limits of the universe (Chico again) to a medical referral in Oakland.

One weekly visit stood out. She had been in the waiting room where she overheard some teenage clients happily discussing their new *"Spirit Guides"*. These were specific animals that they consulted in dreams or trance for key decisions. One boy had his own talking fox while the other had a helpful raccoon.

Teaching them how to do this was a technique I learned from Eduardo Duran's work in Indian Country near Fresno. Supervising him taught me a lot.

Now, some might just say this was only a way to harness imagination in order to generate best choices. Others experienced it literally. Either way, it was valuable, useful, and a definite client mood elevator.

J wanted me to teach her how to have her own Spirit Guide.

I explained that it belonged within a tribal culture with respect. Her own perspective likely wouldn't fit or work.

Hard to say no to J though so: by the end of our hour she had learned the method, left happy.

The following week she entered my office looking confused.

She said: *"It worked okay but my Spirit Guide is human and still alive."*

And: *"It was Eddie Murphy."*

Optional Theme: *I'm a believer* (Eddie Murphy) **https://www.youtube.com/watch?v=R3L6OQWIVhk&ab_channel=P%40S%40f**

Tinder Gold

Theme: *Summer Wine* (Nancy Sinatra, Lee Hazelwood) **https://www.youtube.com/watch?v=791z7Nb985Y&ab_channel=NancySinatra-Topic**

John was now the second president of the first free standing professional psychology school in the nation. And he wasn't a psychologist.

Two of the four founding Campus Deans had forced the departure of the founding president, a very directive Nicholas Cummings. These were Art of the Los Angeles Campus and Maury of the San Diego campus. The founding Campus Dean of the San Francisco campus had left when President Cummings did. That left the founding Campus Dean of the last campus, the Fresno one, a Coptic (Christian) Egyptian named Abou-Ghorra, aka "Abou". He had been loyal to the founding President and was also consequently pushed out by the new one.

Abou in his time there had been teased mercilessly by his peers. Including about the stereotype of Fresno as rural. It was not a coastal community like the other three campuses and had a much smaller population to draw from for its students. So it drew from the world and had the most international composition. Abou endured this, dealing with the teasing by frequent use of an Egyptian saying, translated as *"Let the dogs bark!"*

While at San Francisco, I had joined the other campus administrators at Abou's home for a quarterly meeting. He had provided a great middle-eastern meal for us that evening, with a promise of what sounded like *"belly dancers"* to come after.

Turned out that we had misheard Abou. The dancers were *"ballet dancers"* from a Fresno elementary school. Following this performance, Abou ended the evening as 8 PM was his bedtime.

He was actually a fine friend and I missed him. But the Fresno stereotype had been solidified.

Moreso from Art as he seemed to me the essence of Hollywood when we visited the Los Angeles campus. His pronouncements were passionate, dramatic, loud. I began yelling *"cut!"* or *"scene!"* at times but this didn't go over well.

Maury was dean at the San Diego campus, a marine and navy center. He stereotypically presented himself therefore as an admiral: direct, non-democratic, forceful. His wife governed with him there and, as in the military, her spousal orders were to be obeyed as well. Their governing style wasn't popular with the psychology faculty or students there.

Art and Maury were brilliant and decent people in their own way. Still, they had chafed at the directive style of founding President Cummings. And led the coup that pushed him out. Who to replace him with? Art and Maury decided that the new president should be an academic that was NOT a psychologist. Somebody who therefore would defer to them by virtue of their greater discipline and know-how. State's rights for the campuses.

They hired John as the new president. He had been an administrator at a small women's school. John had impressed them as a hard-headed business-savvy person who would leave them alone and just raise money, like they thought a president should. Once installed as president, John sacked all of them.

I had known the founders when I was one of the San Francisco founding faculty and a Faculty Dean there for four years in the 1970s. In the early 1980s, I returned for another four years as a dean at the Fresno campus, midway between San Francisco and Los Angeles but far too far away from both. Also, Fresno is near three great national parks. Plus the friendly people, and international clientele.

President John, as a welcome, invited me to join him and the different Campus Deans from the ones I had known. We would meet at a pricey Italian Inn and restaurant up in the hills by his home. I was decades younger than the rest, often the only one to order dessert. Maybe it was John's idea of hazing. After the meal, still at table, he reminded all present of my San Francisco founding experience at the school, before *"ascending to your current height at Fresno"* (group laughter). *"So, though this is your first visit to this Inn, draw now upon the magic you absorbed from the hippies in San Francisco and tell us the founding story of this Inn."*

Silence. Then I agreed. Closing my eyes, I simulated a brief trance. Then I announced that the long deceased founder had shared his story. This is what I told them.

"*I was in Italy, young and reckless, even in that terrible winter. I surely had way too much wine in the pub that night. So, as my host and I viewed the most challenging mountain in the Alps through the bay window, I promised that I would climb it the next day. No big deal. Our much older host warned me that it had never been climbed in the winter. I just said: "Overdue then" and laughed.*"

"*The next morning I woke to see that our host had assembled all my gear and was ready to help me fail in my climbing folly. A great breakfast helped and soon I stepped into the chill sun for the ascent I had promised.*"

"*It went well on the climb, against all odds. The mountain had not looked so large from a distance but it had taken the whole day to get to the top. Once there at the peak, I could see the setting sun to the west and, on the other side, a broad dark cloud covering the sky. And moving closer.*"

"Exhausted, I moved down from the peak, not far away, to a plateau. I had twisted an ankle. It was always easier to climb up than to go back down."

"I knew my host would send a party to get me back if I was still gone in the morning. No way could I make a descent on my own, especially in that wild night. It was dark by then and the menacing cloud had arrived. The wind bought horizontal rain, then snow, then hail like bullets. Not weather any help would risk either so I looked for shelter. Stay the night then."

"I found a mound with what looked like a rotted wood door. Using the little strength I had left I managed to pry it open. Inside was what looked like the barren remains of a cottage. Not much left. A fire pit but no kindling, no logs. I had matches but nothing to burn. The freeze seeped in and I shivered."

"With the devastated door pulled closed, the chill remained. And I was soaking wet from the storm. I searched for tinder. Finally, buried at the far and shadowed end of the floor was an iron trunk sticking out an inch or two. It took an hour to get it out and open."

"Inside was what looked like a fiddle. Sort of too old and dusty to play though it did have a violin bow alongside. Too bad I lacked the talent to play it, if it still could after all these years. The wood looked elegant somehow, despite its age. There was a dusty label on the fiddle's underside with a name, presumably the long gone owner."

"I would have liked to keep the old thing but by now the chill was bone deep. Deciding to survive for the morning, I took the fiddle to the fire pit and set it ablaze. With grace the old wood burned slowly and with heat. Soon it was warmer in that small space. I survived the night."

"The morning was clear and sunny. The rescue party got me down to the Pub I had left the day before. I had to borrow some money from my host to pay them. He wondered out loud if I had found any gold up there to pay him back."

"Nope. Just a fiddle but one that saved my life. I still had its owner's name from the fiddle's under side in my pocket and decided to find him or his heirs and thank them for this sacrifice. I showed the name to my host. Surprising me, he laughed and said I was more of a fool than he had thought. Then no more would he say."

"I left the next day. Stopping at pubs, inns, street fairs, telling my story and asking after the owner's whereabouts. Nobody would say though many were amused. Some comforted me for no obvious reason. One said I was better off not knowing."

"I spent more than two months looking for the owner to apologize for burning his fiddle as tinder but thank him for it saving my life. I left Italy without finding him, a man the label said was named "**Antonio Stradivari**"."

"I did eventually learn that my tinder had likely been an original Stradivarius worth many millions of dollars. Well, my life is worth more. To me. But I vowed to raise the money another way. And in these California hills, I built this high priced Inn."

Perhaps inspired by my story of lost opportunity, President John then asked me to order the wine. All there knew I didn't drink and, as the waiter stood by my chair, anticipated my embarrassment.

I scrutinized the expensive multi-page wine list carefully. Then I ordered bottles for the table with confidence. The waiter was pleased, very respectful, as he took my order. He said my taste was superbly excellent and I had ordered the very best wine they owned.

When we were served, all but me sampled the wine and agreed.

Finally, John asked me how I could possibly have known what to order.

Since he was paying for our meal, I decided to tell him: "*Well, to help the owner in the quest for his tinder's gold, I just ordered by far the most expensive one on the list.*"

And it was.

Except For Your One Day

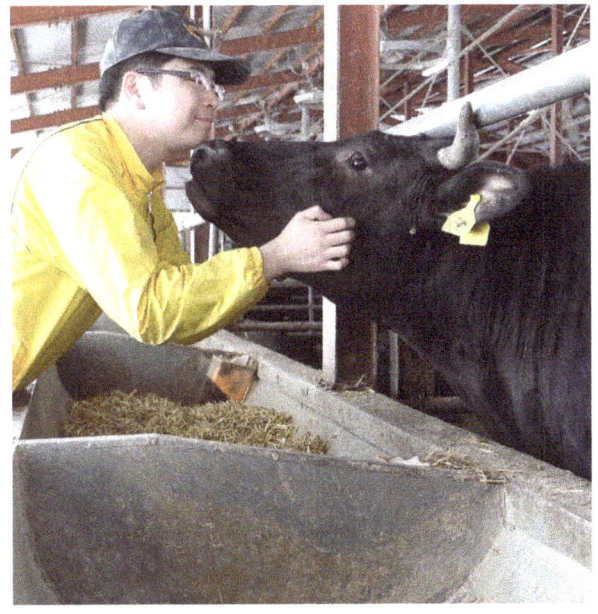

Optional Theme: *Cattle Call* (LeAnn Rimes) **https://www.youtube.com/watch?v=3sP4eQmOt08&ab_channel=suswiee**

In the 1960s, I was a psychologist at the Hawaii State Hospital. I was also a Field Assessment Officer for a Peace Corps project based in Molokai.

On Molokai, three months of training were needed before the two years of service planned for graduating trainees to become Peace Corps Volunteers (PCVs) on remote Pacific Islands. Some of these island nations were so isolated and unique that anybody stepping on the shadow of the King or Queen would be executed.

Lots to learn for the trainees before going there. In one, the live royal bride had been buried with her deceased husband. Something my own wife and I agreed was not for us, even if a dead wife exacted the same tribute from her live husband.

In another remote island culture, the home of the king was considered to be an extension of his body. You could enter his home through the front with his permission and then be swallowed into his generous care. But entering through the rear entrance was considered a form of anal rape, dealt with by instant execution.

Even in large modern and sophisticated island cultures like the Maori of New Zealand, there were family stories of ancient cannibalism. Those stuck out tongues in battle were saying how delicious their enemies would soon be. A woman I knew there still had her grandmother's recipe for pickled thumbs.

Well, one day I had the opportunity to visit a very remote island far from Hawaii, one completely new to me. I was to consult with a psychiatrist there and explore the rest of the time.

The psychiatrist had taken his training further than most in his occupation and knew how to assist his patients with solutions to their issues. He was himself of the indigenous island culture and had integrated it into his practice.

Turned out he was looking more to teach than to learn, which was fine with me. Though I sensed he wanted support for his approaches.

Like many other Pacific cultures, the earth had only two locations: "Here" and "Off-Island". I was an ambassador from "Off-Island", aka the rest of the earth. A grand responsibility.

He first had me sit in on an intake with a young married couple. It was a mixed marriage with the wife native to the island and the husband a white American, formerly of the U.S. Navy. They had been married for a few years already and the husband reported that they both were highly satisfied with each other the whole time. The wife only nodded in agreement but otherwise said nothing. In fact, she was not talking to him at all.

He had been found out having sex with another woman. His wife hadn't spoken to him or anybody else since. Her problem was what to do about it. His problem was how to regain the happiness they had before his brief adventure.

In this culture, marriage might include more than one wife but never sex with anybody but a wife.

Before marriage, sex was very positive and freely granted to consenting partners. After: nobody else but the wife or husband.

A little like the island culture of Yap where women were often topless but as adults were never supposed to expose genitalia.

On this more isolated island, it had been necessary for this American husband to learn where the lines of never were. And he thought he had. Yet, here he was.

The psychiatrist completed our intake by agreeing to take the case. He assigned the wife to meet with him for a private session and the husband to meet with me for his private session. We would all return for a closure session after that. I was apparently to learn by doing.

My mystery to solve was why the husband had risked hurting his wife in such a rare no-complaint-from-either-partner marriage. It didn't take long.

He said he was from Louisiana. He had a culture of his own. Men were understood by women to stray though the wives were not expected to take the same path. He knew how he was supposed to act. He said his wife made him happy in every way. He had hoped to keep his affair secret, near impossible on an island.

So: Why?

He invoked an ancient question. *"Why would I go out for a hamburger when I could have steak at home?"* His answer? *"Variety. Try something new."*

And? How did it work out? *"Not worth it. Wound up hurting her. And no peace for me ever since."*

He went on more about what he had lost. He eventually understood what a deep sacred commitment marriage was on this island. The issue was not really as much about sex, but more about trust. And about caring for her feelings. Finally he resolved to explain himself to her when we met again. To ask for a fresh start. Good progress for an hour.

We all met again. She was still silent but seemed calmer somehow.

The psychiatrist smiled at me. Then asked if either partner had something to say. I looked to the husband and nodded. The husband cleared his throat and began saying how wonderful she was and how he missed what they had. He asked for a second chance.

Silence.

Then he tried to explain his affair with the variety quote: Hamburger over Steak.

Now the silence was tense.

Like an old Frankenstein movie, the air in the room rippled with menace.

After a few seconds, the psychiatrist spoke.

"Speaking of hamburgers and steak, Wagyu beef from Japan is the best you can get. Great marbling. The lucky cows are grass fed and they get beer to help their appetite. They each get a massage every day, along with sake to drink and soothing music. Same when raised in America except they also get to roam free during the day. Though corners may be cut. So in Japan or in America, each and every day of their life is perfect."

The rest of us looked puzzled at this but nobody interrupted. He resumed.

"Perfect except for that one day. Their last day. The day they die, get butchered, and progress to tasty beef."

He now looked hard at the husband. *"Your wife has decided to grant you that second chance. Until now you were her hero. You are not from here and may not have understood our ways. She will feed you well and again make you happy each day of your life together. BUT. Now it is time for you to know a very important thing. If you chose to make the same mistake again, THAT will be your last day."*

The husband was silent as this sunk in.

Now his wife was smiling.

The Pattern's Suspect List

Optional Theme: *Searchin'* (The Coasters) **https://www.youtube.com/watch?v=PN307ssGLuc&ab_channel=Lex187videoz**

"If the shoe fits, it will hurt." Hans Toch, *Iatrogenics Handbook* (2005)

The year was 1972, the place San Francisco. Two female students sat in my office distraught. They had shut the door. Not far from their PhD in psychology at our professional school, they were deeply concerned. Three of the faculty were followers of Freud and therefore identified lesbian women like these two as at best stuck in a childhood phase where girls remained with girls, eventually shunning heterosexuality. At worst these same professors might see their sexual identity as pathology and drop them from the school. I assured them that they were secure. This was San Francisco after all. And I guaranteed that nobody would be expelled at my school for that reason. Most faculty were not Freudian though the few that were psychoanalytic all knew to be fair, valuable, and honorable. Somewhat reassured, the students left.

But I decided I should do something to make these students more secure.

In my other job, clinical psychologist at a San Francisco mental health center, one of my colleagues was psychiatrist Dr. Josette

Mondanaro. She was a charismatic woman who was pioneering a successful program for heroin-addicted pregnant mothers such that they moved to methadone in time for their babies not to be born as heroin addicts. These healthy "Methodone Babies" were even more developmentally advanced than normal babies, possibly an effect of Josette's superb therapeutic guidance for their mothers. Not long from her medical training, Dr. Mondanaro's career would soon have a meteoric rise, resulting in a 1989 seminal book on treating drug-addicted women plus a huge leadership role in generating women's health care centers. In a few years she would be a Deputy Director of California's state drug treatment office. For awhile (another story).

Josette was an advocate for lesbian women and so good a friend that she agreed to come to my professional school and teach a course on drug treatment, plus, along the way, organize the lesbian and bisexual female students, reducing their fears of expulsion. In all of this she was very successful. Way more than expected.

Betty was a PhD student at our school in the Mondanaro era. She had successfully completed her coursework. Now she was ready to present her final doctoral dissertation findings to the community.

Her best friend, Ruth, had done this the week before with the topic *"Being 40 and a Single Woman"*. A time for very self-referential work.

Betty decided to seek the patterns predicting a therapist's sexual abuse of their patients. Betty may or may not have had this experience herself but she certainly knew enough women who had been abused, enough for a large interview cohort and a doctoral dissertation. The pattern seemed to predict patient abuse from a very specific group of therapists, shrinking the suspect list considerably for that time and that place. So her revealing evening presentation was much anticipated.

Betty reserved our largest room for her evening revelation. The students themselves had chosen the furniture, consisting mainly of Harem floor pillows (San Francisco after all). Betty did move in a three seat traditional couch by the front right wall, near her lectern. She reserved this for three of the faculty's senior and popular mentors: Drs. Appel, Bilmes, and Talkoff. Somewhat older than most of the rest of this young faculty, a few assumed she was merely showing respect. Hard for many elders to get up from floor pillows.

Betty had a full room for her performance. The three elder faculty were in their couch places of honor. The rest of us secured a Harem pillow seat or stood.

Eventually, following a literature review, method specifics, examples of abuse from her victim interviews Betty revealed the emergent abuser predictive pattern. These would be therapists who were middle aged, divorced, and with neatly trimmed beards:. They would also be psychoanalysts following Freudian methods (what I had termed in earlier years elders in the *"Freudian American Round Table Society"* for its acronym).

Following a dramatic pause, Betty turned to the three senior bearded divorced Freudian faculty on the couch. Then her audience did the same.

None of these three had actually been found to have abused their patients. Still, Betty's pattern had described them well, shrinking the community suspect list to three men on our couch. Their innocence was not relevant to Betty.

Dr. Appel responded with inspired humor, covering his ears. Dr. Bilmes caught on and covered his eyes, whispered to Dr. Talkoff who, puzzled, covered his mouth as requested by Bilmes. The audience laughed; Betty did not.

Most saw these three mentors as these:

Some, with greater respect, saw them this way:

We had learned that every pattern has its exceptions. And mercy for the innocent on any suspect list. Plus, our faculty had a sense of humor. Essential in a therapist.

One year to the month after the two lesbian students had been to my office, two other female students entered, also distraught. They said they were under great pressure from other women in the program to be have intercourse with another female student, "sex with a sister", and declare themselves to be lesbian. Or at least bisexual. They chose not to do so as they were both heterosexual, only attracted to men, and now feared peer pressure to leave the program. I reassured them that they were safe. Suggested they identify their heterosexual identity as a minority one (for this group) and assert diversity of expression. They agreed. Josette Mondanaro was always an over-achiever.

Dr. Mondanaro with daughter

Note: From Eden E. Mondanaro, Josette's daughter: *"Dr. Josette Mondanaro passed away Christmas Day, 2003, and, true to form, donated her body to science for medical students to learn from. Although the true effect of her work is hard to quantify, tens of thousands of success stories are testimony to how the lives of many mothers, children, and now grandchildren have been quite literally saved over the years. I am always honored and moved by the requests to appear and accept an award or dedication in her name. Total strangers, speaking in the most urgent tones, are constantly reminding me of the depth, courage, and love that this woman possessed. She was to me simply Mom, a single mother who, unbelievably, found the time, strength, and energy to raise me to the best of her abilities.* **"For Those with No Voice of Their Own, She Will Be Sorely Missed***," reads her epitaph. For in the final analysis, hers is a legacy of love, and her spirit will be alive for generations to come."*

Targeted

Optional Theme: *Ghost Riders in the Sky* (Willie Nelson & Johnny Cash) **https://www.youtube.com/watch?v=nOWjX4BpC24&ab_channel=HighwaymenVEVO**

Anti-Psychiatry and Max Fink

I was housebound for a few years but my Home Health Care physical therapist succeeded in aiming for me to be free-at-last. Still, email has given me access to (free) consulting with Stanford experts from home.

Even the last stand at hospice-equivalent home settings should not include suffering. Some interesting pain killer choices, otherwise prohibited, are often allowed. If your cardiologist can refer you to a dental surgeon in your region specializing in cardiac patients, or at least include them in their practice, that may be a pain relief option.

I do often enjoy scuffles with physicians whose credentials represent their only successes. (Max Fink in his books on Electroshock and psychiatry history warned of three deadly *"anti-psychiatrists"* and I was honored to be the one chosen from psychology). The other two were Oakland CA neurologist John Friedberg and Peter Breggin whose psychiatric practice included challenging the iatrogenic pathology of other psychiatrists. We all opposed the destructive continued use of electroshock treatment (ECT) (Morgan 1999).

Ron Howard won an Oscar for his powerful movie "*A Beautiful Mind*". The fatal flaw in this movie was having Dr. Fink as his medical consultant. The movie was based on an actual patient diagnosed a schizophrenic who, with his beautiful mind, was able to reason his way back to sanity. Without drugs. Ex-patient advocate and my anti-ECT warrior friend Leonard Frank told me that Fink had convinced Howard that this key aspect of the story could lead to lawsuits if it led to patients skipping their meds. So the movie ended with a lie, thanking psychiatric medications for the patient's success. Reversing the great accomplishment of the movie's hero completely.

Former patient networks launched complaints. I did too, at least appreciating the appropriateness of Max's last name.

Bert Karon, Ph.D.

Bertram P. Karon, Ph.D., was a Professor of Clinical Psychology at Michigan State University, where he taught since 1962. He is a past President of the Division of Psychoanalysis of the American Psychological Association, and President of the Michigan Psychoanalytic Council. He was selected by the New York Society for Psychoanalytic Training for their 1988 Distinguished Psychoanalyst Award, and their 1982 Outstanding Publication Relevant to Psycho-analysis Award for the book *Psychotherapy of Schizophrenia: The Treatment of Choice*. He was also selected for the 1990 Fowler Award for Distinguished Graduate Teaching by the American Psychological Association Graduate Students and for the 1990 Master Lecturer Award by the

Michigan Psychological Association. He had over 100 publications in American and European journals of Psychoanalysis, Psychology, and Psychiatry.

I met Bert just at the end of a MSU event in which Malcolm X spoke. When the white stage moderator interrupted Malcolm by saying *"Sorry, but your time is up"*. Malcolm took the microphone back and said *"MY time is up?"* and the audience cheered.

I saw what looked like another student afterwards, dressed in a sweater and jeans, surrounded by a group of students. Not much older than me, he was explaining *"what Malcolm X really meant"*. I broke in and said, maybe too aggressively, *"I think he said EXACTLY what he meant. Why is any interpretation needed from you?"* To this, the man in the sweater had a surprising reaction. He smiled and said *"We should talk. Who are you?"* That was Bert's way- to get his attention you needed to challenge him, an approach I had a large supply of at the time.

When I found out he was a new psychology professor I anticipated trouble but, of course, we became good friends. I wound up auditing all his courses that quarter, including ones I'd already had.

I wasn't the only one. Bert was committed to Freud's perspective although he used it in a new way with profoundly psychotic patients. Successfully (Karon & VandenBos, 1981).

This meant his lectures were peppered with erotic language and inferences. Consequently his classes became ever more popular with undergraduates prioritizing the same issues. His first quarter term of teaching, the class had 40 students. The next it had 250. The next one after that had to be held in the football stadium.

In addition to bootlegging the clinical psychology curriculum (a closed shop otherwise) in this way, meaning with Bert's welcome, I also learned a certain style of teaching that I soon modeled in my own career. Maybe with smaller classes of graduate students. As I had done with Hans Toch.

Bert had married a woman who already had a young pre-school child. In class he told us the boy had come running to him crying, saying a bully his age had hit him. Bert suggested that a behavioral specialist might say not to reinforce the crying behavior. Instead that's exactly what he had done. After a comforting hug, the little boy went back out and knocked down the bully. Bert Karon gave the points to Freud over Skinner.

His colleague was a famous social psychologist, Milton Rokeach. Rokeach had just released his new book *The Three Christs of Ypsilanti*. In it he presents the cases of three delusional men, each one of which insisting he was Jesus. Rokeach volunteered his time at their mental hospital so he could bring all three together as a group. Eventually, as friends, they supported each other's delusion, explaining that each was a reincarnation of the other. Rokeach used this as an illustration for his theories of group impact on belief systems. He was not a clinical psychologist and had not helped them to recover. To this criticism he simply alleged that they were all beyond help, incurable. Bert Karon then volunteered time to the same Michigan hospital himself. Affronting Rokeach, Karon cured the lead Jesus, returning him to normal functioning and discharge.

I remember him in my first ProSeminar as a graduate student. In this class each faculty member had one session to introduce their self and their work to us. Rokeach had already been accused by a few of his graduate students of publishing their work under his name. He began his session by saying that clinical psychologists over-complicated research. His example was: If you want to know what most people are afraid of, *"Just ASK them!"* The next class meeting was hosted by Bert Karon. He was asked what he thought of the Rokeach example. He gave what I think of now as a very existential answer: *"If you just ASK what people are afraid of, they will name things like spiders, snakes, heights. But if somebody puts a gun to their head, they will pet the spider and the snake after climbing a high ladder to do it. What frightens people the most is not often a conscious fear."*

He was actually more of a thorn in Max Fink's side than I was. Certainly much earlier. He spent his whole professional life arguing effectively against destructive iatrogenic methods of treatment, especially ECT which he called to my attention before anybody else. His publications and commentary continued years after his paralysis.

Bert was in an auto accident that nearly killed him. I had called his university department to see how he was recovering. He department head said *"His body no longer does what he wants it to do."* Bert was home from the hospital. He was as alert and articulate as ever but his paralysis from the neck down was pretty complete. His wife was no longer living, so no help there. He had some Dragon software installed in his computer and now dictated his work to the machine. He still had much of value to say. For many more years.

I didn't know at first that he and Hans were close, former college roommates, but it makes sense now.

I had hoped to bring him into my conversations with Hans but time ran out for Bert way too early.

At our age, health can shrink the size of our immediate universe and in this way opportunities also diminish until eventually achieving zero.

Bert kept his universe expanding until the very end.

And that's what we all are trying as well.

The Primary Client

Optional Theme: *The Good, the Bad, and the Ugly* (Danish National Symphony Orchestra) **https://www.youtube.com/watch?v=enuOArEfqGo&ab_channel=DRKoncerthuset**

Where I grew up, hockey was the main game we played, even if we did it in a corner ice-covered vacant lot. Not owning any ice skates, I always got to be the goalie. Blocking shots that should not succeed may have been a pattern in my adult life as well. (I did suggest once to a friend, Paul Trautman, that golf might be more interesting if, like in soccer or hockey, a goalie stood in front of each hole. He replied "No need. An invisible goalie is already blocking my shots every time I hit the ball.")

In more than five decades of university and professional school teaching, only rarely have privileged students attempted to make their grades as upwardly mobile as they were. These three blocked shots stand out.

Andorra

In the Pyrenees Mountains between Spain and France, Andorra is the 16th-smallest country in the world by land and the 11th-smallest by population. Its capital is the highest capital city in Europe, at an elevation of 3,356 feet above sea level. Although its main official source of revenue comes from tourism, Europeans had often spoke of its reputation as a smuggling paradise, situated as it is high between two large countries. Possibly because of its elevation, isolation, and other factors, Andorra has claimed the highest life expectancy in the world at 81 years. This particularly intrigued me.

So I had often included this little country as a place I would love to visit, explore, and understand.

I was therefore pleased when one of my students in an undergraduate course introduced himself as from Andorra. He said he was from the wealthiest and most influential family there, and was to complete his education here in the United States.

All went well for him until the final exam in which he earned a "C" or average grade, giving him the same grade for the course. This concerned him as he told me that his parental approval to stay in our country was contingent on getting only "A" or "B" grades in every class he took.

So he asked me how much money would I accept to raise his grade to an "A" or, if need be, to a "B".

Remembering the smuggler ethos reputed to his culture, I explained very gently that in my country such bribes were not allowed. I cautioned him to not attempt this with any other faculty as an American student would surely be expelled for offers like that.

He looked annoyed at first, then curious. I had to affirm twice more that I would not raise his earned grade for any amount of money. But I did ask him why he was so puzzled.

"First time here I've been turned down" he said. And walked out.

Never did find out any specifics from him on prior bribes.

I added Andorra to a mental list of places I was unlikely to be welcomed to.

Israel

Israel is a larger and far more diverse country than Andorra. On the one hand, there is a strong Peace Movement in a progressive faction while, on the other hand, there is a strong right wing traditionalist movement. While all adult Israelis have mandatory military experience, there are ones who stay to pursue a military career.

One of these, a high ranking military officer, was completing a psychology doctoral program at the California Graduate School where I was the Academic Vice President.

He was waiting for me in my office, sitting in the visitor chair, looking tense.

This was unusual. The chair was by design very comfortable. Students and other visitors, until this time, visibly relaxed in its arms.

(A former colleague at a conference asked me if I still had that *"wonderful relaxation chair"* as she had always been so comfortable that she hated to leave my office. I told her that, no, I got rid of it. "But *WHY*?" she asked. People stayed too long I explained.)

The officer explained that he only had a few months to complete his requirements before he was mandated to return to service in Israel. This time limit was not flexible, he insisted.

The problem was that he had failed to pass a comprehensive exam by a single question. It was so close, he had to ask, given his unique circumstances if I would just drop that question from his exam and by that allow him to pass the requirement.

He had been to the president of the graduate school with the same request but that dignitary had said it was up to me, my call. (Sigh.)

I explained that to do so would be unethical and unfair to the other graduate students. Instead I suggested Plan B. Per our rules, he could request and schedule a retest in a month, before which I could find him a mentor to coach him on how to raise his performance. This should not be hard given how close he had been to passing.

He refused and stormed out of my office.

He carried his complaint against my decision to the president, then to the Board, then to the Faculty Chair. All these efforts failed. His week had been devoted to this.

Now he sat once again in my office. This time he sat relaxed in the comfortable chair.

He had requested a retest, per the rules, and wanted to now follow my Plan B. He was sure that with hard work he would pass next time (he did).

He thanked me for my academic ethics, said he respected everything I had said.

I said that Plan B would be fine. But why all the struggles if he agreed with me?

The Israeli Officer looked surprised. Explaining: *"Well of course I had to know that I had exhausted every possible opportunity to win before I conceded the issue."* And *"Nothing personal. I respected your decision from the beginning."*

California

He was in one of the earliest pre-doctoral cohorts at the first free-standing professional school of psychology's San Francisco campus. He was intense, outspoken.

He was also a very bright contrarian. Anything required of him usually led to his immediate rejection. This happened on the first day in my first class with his cohort in their first year of classes.

The initial assignment was to write a paper on advocacy, a core competence on how to make productive change. He objected immediately: *"We're here to learn, not to be forced to write more years of pointless papers. This is a dumb idea!"*

I didn't see much agreement in the other graduate students, most experienced in the field and often older than me. I did see interest in how I would handle this obnoxious challenge. Okay then.

"All right. We are a campus that tries new approaches. You may choose to write this paper instead on why you think it's a dumb assignment."

Laughter in the class.

He agreed. It was a good paper. A fair example of advocacy. Though it was also advocacy for himself. The cohort was satisfied. So was I. The class went well from that point on. It was a few years before I realized I had made a big mistake.

He completed all his academic classes in good order. By his last year in the psychology PhD program he had only to complete a new pre-doctoral internship and his doctoral dissertation.

I was a member of his three-person faculty dissertation committee. In the planning meeting he proposed doing a "theoretical thesis" dissertation which would have been all discussion, something he did well. I insisted he instead gather actual data as evidence for an original idea or contribution to the field. Psychology is primarily an evidence-based science. He balked of course but the other two faculty agreed with me so it was decided. He agreed to comply.

I wasn't his dissertation chair so he worked with another faculty member who had that honor. In a few months his dissertation chair let us know his draft was done and we could schedule an oral defense to complete the process. This defense, reflecting the counter-culture nature of our innovative pioneer psychology school, was this time to be held on a Sausalito houseboat. The rules called for us to have at least a month to read and review his draft manuscript. But of course he gave it to us the day before his orals, no apology. I read it that night though I doubt the other two faculty did, given the time squeeze.

The first thing that I noticed was that the numbers in the abstract didn't match the numbers in the text. As Yul Brynner's King of Siam role made famous on the Broadway stage: it was definitely a *"puzzlement"*.

He showed up in the houseboat, dressed formally, and carrying a bottle of champagne plus four ornate glasses. Clearly he planned for us to all celebrate once the defense was done.

Once he had very briefly summarized his dissertation, I asked the first question. Why didn't the abstract match the text?

He turned red in the face and snapped *"I TOLD you I didn't want to collect any data! So I made the numbers up! Satisfied now?"*

I was not. I refused to sign his approval. He did not pass. The other two faculty tried to mediate, suggesting he might just do a new thesis. At this he rose and walked out of the houseboat. Yes, and he took his champagne bottle and glasses with him.

On arriving at the campus the next day, I learned that he had also been caught forging his internship field placement supervisor's signature on the weekly attendance sheets. In fact the placement had been delayed from opening but he had pretended that he had been going anyway.

So, bright as he was, he had a pattern of cheating. No apology or regret was forthcoming. His position was that he had put in the years, passed his classes, and paid the tuition. What was the problem?

Any of this today would justify immediate expulsion. That was my choice even then. But it required the approval of my own supervisor, the Campus Dean.

A few of the faculty ignored his obvious character disorder and urged that he be given another chance, maybe some psychotherapy first.

The Campus Dean privately agreed with me but wanted me to set up some sort of review panel to mollify the forgiveness faculty. Maybe an equal number of un-conflicted faculty and students. I could chair it without vote.

I met with him. He was sure this would exonerate him and cooperated. We agreed on three specific faculty and three specific students who would be fair to join me as Chair. The review panel commenced its work.

His cheating was confirmed immediately. Yet our panel's weekly meetings on how to respond went on and on for some time.

Of course, the Watergate hearings were being televised at the same time. Seeing our national president being held accountable was national news that continued too. It clearly influenced our local process, although any of the panel's fiercely independent faculty or students at the time would certainly not agree that this was so.

Our president, Nick Cummings, had once asked me who I thought the school's primary client was. Stakeholders like faculty, administration, and staff were not the answer. Nor was it the Board of Trustees or the administration. No, not even the students we were training, the ones we had selected and saw as in our care. Not our financial donors or contributors. Not the accreditation agencies.

No, our primary client for this clinical psychology training school should be the patients our graduates serve, once we grant these new psychologists our doctoral degree. We had an obligation not to graduate any new practitioners that were lacking proficiency, or even ones that could damage the people they treat. First of all, do no harm.

When Nick Cummings first told me this, it made perfect sense. The situation he was addressing at the time was my decision as Faculty Dean to remove an impaired unproductive faculty member, and to hire a competent substitute. There had been a review panel of faculty and students then too, one divided between forgiveness and removal. The primary client was seen by them as either the impaired faculty member or the students that depended on him. That time the review panel was advisory to me. The divided panel chose forgiveness by a single vote, recommending that I retain the faculty member unable to do his job.

I thanked them for their advice, walked the faculty member on a one way trip to the door, said goodbye, and hired a new person who could actually do the job.

Within a month of the arrival of the new high performance faculty member, all of the review board thanked me for my decision, one favoring the students. I told them I had actually decided this in favor of their future patients, the primary clients of the school. People deserving fully trained, highly competent, practitioners.

President Cummings had helpfully clarified this higher priority. Recalling this, it suggested a solution for the current issue with the dissertation student. The Campus Dean liked my idea. Surprisingly, so did the student, confident of his sure and certain triumph. The idea: I promised him that he could graduate if *all* the faculty and students on the review panel, not including me, would sign a letter affirming that on graduation he would be a competent clinical psychologist, one they would be willing to recommend or refer people to him for his services. He and I signed an agreement for this.

Nobody on the review board would sign the letter endorsing this student as being a competent psychologist. They all cared about our primary client.

Or, as some later said, they cared too about any consequent vicarious legal liability for any of his destructive future actions. He was then expelled with no doctoral degree.

Years later I heard that he, after being expelled without the degree, had claimed he had the degree after all. He tried to practice without it but disappeared when complaints brought in law enforcement. Forgiveness is wasted on psychopathy.

So that was that. Until a decade later.

I was at a state psychology convention when I spotted the same former student, older now, with a name tag that had "*Dr.*" on it. As we walked toward each other, for a second I wondered if he had matured and forgiveness was actually in order these many years later. Maybe a second chance had worked for him?

When he spotted me, he stopped a few feet away. He scowled. Said: "*Yes, I got this doctorate from a diploma mill, paid a lot for it. All this took me an extra ten years and every second of that was YOUR fault. I dream about killing you by running you over with my car. What do you think about THAT?*"

I just said "*Well, even in your dreams you need a CAR to do that?*"

He frowned and considered my words. Psychologist and friend Leland Van den Daele described much of what I say as "time release". This applied here. I laughed, moved on.

Now in our 21st Century

Were these three individuals from the 20th century preview of the massive psychopathy we contend with today? Is it now legitimate for huge proportions of people to allege the opposite of what is known as true? Are untrue, even absurd, *"alternative facts"* okay for some if they accomplish a goal, achieve a win?

How do we choose to deal with this? For me, the primary client of our time is the next generation. What better world will we leave them? We, collectively and individually, can choose to contribute answers.

Max Returns: Ray's Next Life

Optional Theme: *Once Upon a Time in the West (*Danish National Symphony Orchestra) https://www.youtube.com/watch?v=efdswXXjnBA&ab_channel=DRKoncerthuset

He did.

"He threw me in lock up for saying "Hey guy." I didn't care because chains are like toys to me. I can take them off almost as fast as they can put them on me. A person that has been locked up as long as I have, things like chains, lock up and prison don't bother that person because he or she is used to it."

(Selected sections excerpted from the 2005 *Iatrogenics Handbook* with permission.)

Normally less than one percent of any institutionalized mental patient population is considered so dangerous that they are involuntarily locked in maximum security. It would be a serious mistake to consider this minority as simply helpless victims of an oppressive treatment system since quite serious crimes often precede their incarceration. On the other hand, the hospital setting, unlike the jail, infers they are to be treated for the personality disorder leading to the violence. Too often staff do not know what treatment to give or, worse, assert there is no effective help possible. Further, who will take the responsibility to risk that someone, already having committed a serious crime, will never commit another?

Max is a pseudonym for a thirty-eight-year-old man incarcerated since the age of fourteen. Abandoned at the age of six months, he was reclaimed and abandoned again by his mother at six years. Receiving a blow to the head from a baseball bat at that age, he developed mild epileptic attacks, since treated effectively with moderate medication.

At fourteen, after some vandalism, he was labeled a juvenile delinquent and found his new home to be a mental hospital.

At eighteen, while on leave, he attacked a man who he insisted came at him with a knife. He was described at that time as having violent outbursts of temper and earned the diagnostic label still with him today: *"anti-social personality, severe"*.

Transferred to the penitentiary, he was charged with the murder of another inmate at age twenty-four. Max said the inmate attacked him and he held him at arm's length by the throat. Max has unusual strength and the other inmate's larynx was fatally crushed. Max was twenty-four.

Max retained his temper and an earned reputation for regularly getting into *"intense oppositional positions with authority figures."*

He mellowed much over the years and became more and more invested in beginning a life on the outside of the institution.

He objected to a perceived lack of meaningful resocialization treatment and the omission of key behavioral signposts leading to an exit. To most residents of his ward, he was seen as congenial and positive.

But, one year, he attempted an escape. In explaining his actions, he said: *"I need a resocialization program. I'm sane, competent, and not dangerous."* The periodic fights he explained with *"No matter what environment you're in, you have to adapt. If not, you're an outcast. I'm acting normally for this environment."*

The staff agreed he was not psychotic, suicidal or homicidal. They did not agree, however, that he was not dangerous.

They felt that in a less-defined environment like the "outside," his rage would be more likely to surface.

Max asked what evidence would be accepted that he is safe ... or is he a perpetual victim of his past?

The staff replied that worse than he have been released (and this is true) but made no specific predictions.

They, in my judgment, were sincere and, if they do cover themselves, they also mean to protect people on the outside. Max wanted to be one of those people on the outside.

Here is an excerpted letter from Max done from those years he was in "max" (maximum security), a stream of consciousness reflecting the range of his perspective and personality in that time and place, *verbatim et literatim.*

"Daily Life in Max

From the day the hospital was opened, it has been against the rules to have sexual relationships with women: visitors or female patients. But it is O.K. to have sex with someone of your own sex. In the hospital's eyes, this is normal. If a man gets caught having sex with a woman, even if she is his own wife, he gets regressed back to rather medium or maximum security. And nothing is done to the female other than maybe a week's restriction or if she is a visitor, restricted from the hospital grounds.

There isn't a maximum security for women. In order to have visitors, the patient must fill out a written request to the ward staff, and it has to be signed by the ward Doctor, ward charge and the track chief. This is done in prison the same way. Also, the visitors are shuck down before they can come in to visit. They are not allowed to bring in anything except a pack of smokes, no lighter or matches, to smoke while visiting the patient. Kissing and hugging is frowned upon and sometimes stopped. Patients are not allowed to have homemade or store bought food or candy of any kind brought into them.

Patients are chained down to the bed with steel hand and leg cuffs, not leather cuffs, for reasons such as, defending themselves, for refusing to put up with verbal abuse from patients and staff, for trying to protect their personal property from thieves, for voicing their feeling or opinions about a wrong that is or has been done to a patient or patients or to themselves, for standing up for the rights of when they are being abused, being harmful to ourselves or others and sometimes just because a staff member doesn't like a certain patient. The overall treatment of a patient is that of a criminal in a prison, not a patient in a hospital.

When a patient starts making waves, by filing writs and lawsuits against the hospital for a release hearing or to sue the hospital, the ward staff and professional staff do their best to make that patient blow up so they can rather regress him back to maximum security or chain him down. Then, when it's time for him to go to court, the hospital can say that he is dangerous. Therefore, they can prevent the patient from getting out.

The longer a patient is kept in confinement, the more money the hospital gets for his keep. How they do this is: they tell the government budget committees and the legislators that they need more money to treat you; they need more experienced doctors and a better treatment program for you in order to properly treat you so you can return to the street a cured man. The patients never receive any of this wonderful treatment that the hospital got the money for. Patients receive nothing in most cases but confinement, abusive treatment and never accepts any more of that. So what you have in most mental hospitals, mainly this one, is a warehouse of nothing but bodies. These are bodies that the outside world could care less about. So, they are warehoused and forgotten and the big wheels that run the regional government rake in the money that is supposed to go for the treatment of these patients or bodies.

In most cases, the hospital staff members make a patient sick or sicker and a lot of times cause non dangerous patients to rather act out in a dangerous manner or become dangerous. The reason for this is: the professional staff and ward staff are so incompetent that they can't diagnose a patient properly for his mental illness if he has any to begin with. But surely there will be more illnesses than he will know what to do with by the time these one-year wonders, crystal ball readers and miracle workers get through brainwashing him with their psychological warfare games. This means, that if the doctor keeps telling the patient that he has a mental illness, and after hearing this from him and ward staff over a period of time, the patient will start believing he has this mental illness, when in fact he hadn't, up until he was brainwashed. But now he becomes sick and becomes a mental illness unto himself. All because the professional staff are too incompetent to do their job efficiently. As for causing a non-dangerous patient to become dangerous, the reason for this is: the staff force a patient into a prison-like setting, so that a patient can run but can't hide from trouble and abuse from patients and staff alike.

So, he is forced to act out in a violent manner even though he isn't violent by nature. But because staff will not aid him when he is being assaulted or abused, to the point that any normal person will fight back, by not doing anything when other patients steal or bulldog him out of his personal property; by chaining him down for defending himself or his property, for standing up for his rights, especially when it's an employee who is abusing his rights. These are just a few things the staff do to patients that make them act out in a violent manner. And when the patient does act out, the staff says he's dangerous.

Patients are not allowed to buy, sell or trade with other patients or employees. Patients are not even allowed to put what little they're allowed to make in a place where visitors can see them and buy them. So, patients without any money can't make money by selling the things that they make to visitors. Selling to visitors is even against the rules.

Patients on maximum security are not allowed to check out books from the library or the law library. Only patients from medium and open wards with privileges outside the fence can use these libraries. So maximum security patients do without.

When a patient is put down in steels. hands and feet are chained to the bed, the ward staff gang up on him. Anywhere from six to ten employees jump on him before they put the steels on and hit, kick, twist legs and arms, neck to the point that they almost break and sometimes do. This isn't done in all cases, but most. Then, when they start chaining him down, they put the cuffs on tight, to where his wrists and ankles start to swell or the steel cuts into the skin. And then they pull the leather belt so tight around his arms and bed that he can hardly move. If he complains, the staff beat on him some more if they don't like him. And the only time you are allowed to use the "john" is when they let you up for your meals. So, if you have "to go" you either do it in your bed or try to lean over enough to do it on the floor.   Myself, I am a locksmith, so I take the chains off of me whenever I want up and then chain myself back down.

This kind of treatment happens to those patients that the staff dislike or when a staff member comes to work with a hard on because his old lady refused to take care of it. So, he comes to work and takes it out on every patient on the ward, but rather than locking them up in their rooms, he aggravates and agitates the patients until one of them can't take any more and voices his dislike about what he is doing. In some cases, it's up to five to six patients that get thrown in their rooms or chained down. You can tell when he is on the ward without even seeing or hearing him because the tension is so thick you can't cut it with a chain saw. When he is on duty, the whole ward is sitting on a case of TNT but when he leaves you can feel the tension go out with him. Then the ward is back to normal. Every ward he has been on, there has been nothing but trouble because of him.

He got stabbed one time by another patient whom he had been agitating for months every day. So the patient had as much as he could take and stabbed him with a piece of steel off a table. If he had had a handle on that shank, he would have killed him. But when he tried to stab him, it only went in a few inches and it slipped out of his hand.

He threw me in lock up for saying "Hey guy." I didn't care because chains are like toys to me. I can take them off almost as fast as they can put them on me. A person that has been locked up as long as I have, things like chains, lock up and prison don't bother that person because he or she is used to it.

The staff have been trying to get me to blow up so they can say and prove that I'm dangerous because that is the only way I can lose the lawsuit I have against the hospital and the District Court approved my lawsuit to be heard. The federal courts don't usually approve a writ that is against the hospital unless that person has a damn good case against it. Most, if not all hospitals, are funded by the federal government so if I win, the federal government will stop funding this place until they get their act straightened out, where this will be a hospital, NOT a prison as it is now.

Group therapy and one-to-one are nothing but a side show for the staff. Patients can't get any help out of these make-believe groups and one-to-ones because the staff only hold these therapies so they can write in the patient's chart that he has been receiving treatment. This is another way the hospital has of beating a patient in court. When a patient files for a release hearing or files a law suit on grounds of not receiving treatment, the hospital shows the court your chart which states that you have been receiving treatment in groups and one-to-one therapies.

So this circus-style side show therapy isn't doing the patients any good because it's nothing but a big joke and that joke is on the patients. They go to these groups and one-to-ones, looking for help and treatment for their problems. They go to them angry and come out angrier.

Patients on maximum security do not and cannot have occupational therapy to help them pass the time of day constructively. If a patient is on medium security, he has to put in a written request to the ward staff to be approved. And then, he has to wait for an opening before he can participate in occupational therapy. This waiting more often than never takes weeks and sometimes months. The reason for this is because the hospital only lets up to ten patients participate at a time, so the patient has to wait until a patient gets transferred to another ward.

The hospital has a gym with a swimming pool, bowling alley, basketball court, billiard room, exercise room with barbells, etc. and a library. But patients that do not have privileges outside of the fence are deprived of these things. These so called privileges are therapy and good treatment for patients but a patient has to earn the right to treatment. So patients on maximum security never get to use these facilities. So, therefore, they are deprived of treatment because they are looked upon as convicts instead of patients.

Maximum security has a small basketball court and a yard of nothing but dirt. But, we are denied daily use of these. Patients are lucky to get outside once a year, and we're lucky to use the gym once a week. The reason for this is because the staff are too lazy to take us out or to the gym. And the recreational therapist is also too lazy. He spends most of his time in the South recreational hall playing pinball machines and other games with the other recreational men, to come over and take our ward, outside or to the gym.

The food is prepared so badly that most of the meals are thrown-up. Ninety percent of it is starch. I'm five foot ten and weigh a hundred and forty-five pounds. I've never weighed over a hundred and forty-nine because the food is too bad for my stomach to hold down. The only times we get good meals are when a holiday comes around or when important visitors come around to inspect the hospital. Most of the ward staff won't eat it.

The ward staff and professional staff, which we don't have many of here, because they're all one-year wonders and incompetent to help themselves, let alone to help the patients. They can't control their emotions, like most people do. So they get a job here where they can take their frustrations, anger and any other problems they have out on the patients. Then they can go back out on the streets after they've put in their eight hours and be almost normal for another sixteen hours.

Patients on maximum and medium security are deprived of a proper educational program because education and vocational rehabilitation is a "privilege", not treatment or therapy, in the eyes of the hospital staff. So, therefore, patients have to earn the right or privilege of a proper education. Patients aren't allowed to attend vocational rehabilitation. Rehab is on the hospital grounds without privileges outside the fence.

These privileges can only be gotten on medium security to further the patient's education by taking a GED or a vocational training.

The ward staff can, and often or mostly do, use foul language when expressing themselves about their dislike about a patient or what he is doing that they don't like: whether it be to them or another patient. But let a patient do the same to the staff and down he goes in steels. It's okay for a staff member to verbalize his or her feelings in whatever way they feel like but not a patient. This also goes for threatening: staff can, but not a patient.

Staff can and often do, mentally and physically abuse patients for pushing the staff too far, but don't let a patient try it. He will not only be chained down, but also get the shit kicked or slapped out of him. In some cases, if the patient gets hurt, he won't get any medical care unless you're too badly hurt or someone feels sorry for you which is very unlikely.

Some patients can do almost anything and get away with it, but let another patient try it and he'll get chained down. Most of the patients here at the hospital get a screwing because of their past record. The hospital holds their past record against them. But let a patient keep bringing up a staff member's past, if he has one, and down he goes in chains.

Most of the staff don't want to do anything like open doors to patients' side rooms, clothes room doors or mop room floors, go to the canteen for the patients, have therapy with patients. All they do most of the time is sit in the office and gossip, play footsies with the female employees, read newspapers or books like Playboy and watch TV and sometimes bulldog it so they can see what they want to watch, play cards and other games with other patients. Things like this is what an employee does with his or her eight-hour shift. They do hold make-believe staffings to consider transfers, treatment programs for patients twice a week in which the patient has no say so on any of the planned treatment the staff have already set up for the patient.

But the staff demands the patients to jump when they say jump. Ward staff and professional staff expect and demand respect from the patients, but they don't believe they have to earn it because they are the employees, and we are patients which in their eyes makes us not equal to them as humans. And, therefore, we don't deserve the same respect. But let a patient or patients try and demand the respect that is due them and all the patients get is: ignored, told in not so good language to shut up. And if he still demands respect that is due him, he gets chained down.

Ward and professional staff want the patients to trust and believe them, but the staff won't trust and believe the patients. How can patients trust and believe in staff that live by a double standard and have proven time after time that they can't be trusted or believed? Not all mental hospital employees are this way but there are enough to make a patient afraid to trust even the nicest employees that work here. There are a few but not that many because they don't last long.

Most of the staff say all kinds of good things about you, to your face, but then they go and write in your chart just the opposite of what they said.

I learned a long time ago, "that a man is only as good as his word." And I have lived by that almost to the tee. And because I have, I'm trusted and believed by those who are the same, and by most who aren't.

The hospital discharges the ones that they know can't make it and have to return for more hospitalization. The staff makes this mistake because they don't have what it takes to be a competent person let alone a competent professional staff member in any hospital.

They think just because a patient does and says what they want him to say and do, that he is ready for the outside world. What these crystal ball readers won't accept is that school and book learning is good to a certain point. But after that you have to put aside the book and use common sense. There are things in life that all the schooling and book learning in the world won't teach you. And one of those things is how to read a human being and tell him what he is going to do in the foreseeable future. You can only guess, and in a lot of cases you will be wrong.

Life in an institution and life in the free world is like daylight and dark. So just because a patient acts like a model patient, or is a model patient in an institution like this hospital or a convict in prison doesn't mean he can or is going to be a model citizen. Because I have seen and did time with both, patients and convicts that were as much as a lamb in confinement but went on a killing spree once they were released.

The only way to find out how a patient or convict is really going to be once he is released, is give him a chance to prove himself by putting him on an open ward with town passes so he can work and be with other citizens or to place him on an outpatient basis. The staff should do this to the patients that they can't prove one way or the other that they can or can't make it. This test should be for six months to a year. And if he can make it for a year, then he can make it for good. But the hospital won't do this to patients that could and can make it, because these are the kind of patients that scare the hell out of them.

Not because the patient is trying to but because the so-called professional staff don't know how to deal with a patient that can't and will not be intimidated, or turned into one of their brainwashed model nuts, that will kiss their ass and make them feel important. I am and always have been one of those patients that they don't know how (and are afraid) to deal with. I don't lie to them, or kiss their asses, and will never be intimidated by them with their chains, lock up, the threat of not getting a transfer or privileges outside the fence, etc. I am freer or should I say that I have more freedom than most people I have ever met. Freedom is a matter of mind, prison is also.

A man can lock another man's body up, but he can never lock his free will and mind up. So man makes his own prison and his own Garden of Eden with his mind. So that's why these people will never intimidate me to becoming one of their brain washed nuts. "I'm free of mind and will."

These kinds of patients are the ones that scare the hell out of them, and they don't know how to deal with them. Someone that tells them like it is and hope they don't like it.

Most patients are intimidated by the hospital. The reason for this, is because the hospital threatens them with maximum security, chains, medication if they don't want treatment or refuse to participate in any of the therapy programs that have been forced on them. So patients are intimidated and they attend any and all the groups and one to one's they are told to attend. And does anything else that he is told to do, if they want to or not, just to get a transfer and privileges.

When this kind of forced treatment or therapy is applied the patient gains nothing if hardly anything, but a transfer and some privileges.

So what good is the hospital system doing for patients that need help, but feel too intimidated to open up to the ones that are hired to help them regain their sanity?

This kind of system is the cause of all the warehousing of patients in the hospital.

And because of this, the heads of the hospital administration and some of the heads of the local government get rich off of the overcrowded patient population. They're getting rich at the expense of patients that need help and can't get it, because of incompetent staff, and money hungry politicians.

The law states: The rights of patients in all mental hospitals are for all patients. whether they're on maximum security or not. But the- real hospital policy has its own laws and rules, and disregards government laws in most cases.

There are too many patient rights to list but the most important ones that the patients on maximum security have are:

Leather restraints are to be used: not steel restraint. But steel restraints (hand and leg cuffs) are always used on maximum.

Physical restraints are only to be used when a patient is an immediate danger to himself or others. and 110 preventive measures are possible without restraints.

Patients on Forensic don't have to do hardly anything to get steels put on them and tied to the bed, even when seriously injured.

Seclusion is only to be used when leather restraints are not necessary to keep patient from hurting himself or others. Maximum patients are locked in seclusion for as little as an employee's bad day or mood.

Restraints and seclusion are not to be used as a disciplinary use. Maximum patients are punished in this manner for little reason at all.

Medical treatment: patients are entitled to psychiatric and medical treatment and care appropriate to his individual needs, while in this facility. Maximum patients only receive medical and psychiatric treatment and care, if and when the ward doctor or staff feels like giving it to them, "even when everyone can clearly see that you need it."

Personal rights: patient has the right to be free from mental or physical abuse on the part of the staff members, other patients and visitors. Maximum patients have no way to protect themselves from abuse from others, staff or patients, because self-defense is against the rules.

Visiting rights: no visiting restrictions are to be put on either the patients or visitors, unless the patient becomes or is a danger to himself or others or to his visitor or the visitor becomes detrimental to the patient's wellbeing. Maximum patients must fill out a visitor's list or request like prisoners do in prison in order to get a visit from anyone, other than immediate family, lawyers, doctors or religious counselors. In some cases, patients have to have their immediate family put on their visiting list before they can visit.

Recreational rights: All patients are to have at least one hour of fresh air and sunshine, if weather permits, if not one hour of recreation in the gym. This recreational right is to be at least once a day.

Maximum patients are deprived of this right because the recreational man and ward staff are too lazy to take us outside or to the gym.

Occupational therapy: patients are to have at least four to six hours of occupational therapy a day. So, they will have something constructive to do during the waking hours of the day. Maximum patients aren't allowed to have any kind of occupational therapy for reasons of: a patient stole a hammer from the O.T. shop, and tried to knock the bricks out of the wall to escape. So, everyone paid for it, over two years ago leaving us short of building space, and short of occupational therapists.

Social rights: insofar as possible, this facility shall attempt to maintain a normal social environment. Maximum patients are treated like convicts and are locked up with convicts. There is very little therapy if any and patients are forced to live in a prison-like setting, instead of a hospital or a normal social environment.

Ventilation, heating and lighting rights: patients are to be housed in a building that is adequately well ventilated, heated and well lighted. Maximum patients are deprived of these rights; the ventilation, heating have never worked. We freeze in the winter and roast in the summer. The lighting is very bad, our windows are eight feet high and three inches wide, this doesn't let much, if any sunlight in at all.

These are the most important patient rights that are being abused on maximum. The things that happen to maximum patients which I have mentioned do not and would not happen outside maximum wards too much or too long, because the outside world, meaning the patients visitors, would put a stop to it. The reason for this is because non-maximum patients are allowed to have their visitors come on the wards, where they can see what goes on in the wards, and are allowed to talk to other patients on the ward, to see and find out how they are treated.

Also, security police are not in charge of the housing of patients and the treatment programs and care of the patients on other wards "like they are on maximum: security first, treatment second!"

This goes for all treatment, medical care on surgery. Maximum patients are chained to the bed by a log chain around their leg while on surgery!

But since the patient's visitors do not see the wards, and how patients are treated, most all the people in the free world think we are treated with all the TLC in the world. Because they can't bring themselves to believe that people are treated like we are in this day and age.

The law states: that all patients, no matter what their commitment, are to be treated as civil commitments. The only exceptions are, transfers from penal institutions and those who have been found guilty of a crime, but not guilty by reason of insanity.

There is one problem the patients of this system have that seems to make our grievances even worse.

This problem is that our patient representative works for the hospital system, not for us. So whenever we have a grievance about our rights or anything else that is against the hospital staff, we can't get anything done. Because we have to go through a person who has and always will back up the system.

Psychological warfare: Harassment; intentional and systematic efforts to elicit strong expression of emotion by means of various forms of provocation.

Frightening patients into conformity ... "This is the number one treatment program."

Dual numbers: it is unlawful to try and convict and then send a mental patient to prison.

The hospital does this and has been getting away with it for God only knows how long. What the hospital does if a patient commits a crime while a patient here at the hospital in most cases is they find the patient sane and competent after he has been filed on. And if the court sends him to prison, the court has sent a mental patient to prison by law, because the hospital has not discharged the patient.

This is called a dual number, which by federal law is against the law. Because the patient is a mental patient until he is fully discharged. And you can't send a mental patient to prison, because mental patients and convicts cannot be confined together.

Patients that have been found not guilty by reason of insanity are not allowed to be transferred out of maximum where all the civil commitments are housed, because we are labeled as criminal commitments by the law and therefore treated as criminals instead of mental patients.

Hospital police carry guns all over the hospital grounds. They carry them in their cars and are stored in their office, where any patient that really wanted a gun could steal one, right out of their car or out of their office. By law no weapons are allowed on State hospital grounds.

Patients who have been sent to the hospital for observation, confinement, treatment, and incompetency are also locked up with convicts from prison.

So, to sum up the trouble with this system and what changes should be made to make it a system that could and would help those in need of help are as follows:

Stop the warehousing of patients to make money.

The only way to stop this abuse to patients, is to have a federal investigation of how this hospital is run. And rather close it down or weed out the incompetent staff and the greedy heads of the government and replace professional staff that will do the job that they are trained and paid for.

Cause so much trouble for the government and the hospital, through the press and other organizations that want and aren't afraid to help put so much heat on the politician and the hospital, that it will cause the concerned people of the outside world to demand a change and get it.

Talk to good and important lawyers, about how patients are deprived of their rights "which I have already mentioned most of these rights," and ask them even if you have to beg them to, to take on the government on behalf of the patients, by filing a class action law suit for as much money as they can get plus a reform of the hospital, so there won't be any more abuse and mistreatment of patients like warehousing. They would have to take the case free, because we don't have the money that most lawyers want. But they would get paid out of the money they made off of the lawsuit.

These are the only ways that can be used to straighten this place up, so that patients in need of help can receive the proper treatment and care."

* * *

I asked a staff member, someone I like and respect, what Max's status really was. He responded: *"It boils down to this: he says he's cured, and he'll kill any son-of-a-bitch that says otherwise."*

I shared his previous quote with Max before going to publish the book, and he responded with a genuine belly laugh.

"Well, it's even worse than that," he said, *"the son-of-a-bitch I'm killing is me! They just won't let me out until I agree that I'm too dangerous to leave. . . .. (laugh) and I'm too stubborn to lie. The most dangerous thing about me right now are my lawsuits! I hope they will be dangerous enough. No, wait a minute, more dangerous than the lawsuits is this: I won't give up on myself. As to the people here, some I care about and some I don't. I don't want to kill them, what I want to do is say goodbye to them. I understand the difference, I'm not sure they do."*

Max had learned the trades of locksmith, jeweler, watch repairman. He had ventilated much of his younger fury, but rage remained. Is it inappropriate? He was seen as lacking insight into the things he does to provoke attack or confinement, but are his criticisms of the system off the mark? The work of Zimbardo, Milgram, and others demonstrate the brutalizing effect on principled staff in an environment in which one group holds total power over another; in which both groups are confronted daily by their failures and inadequately rewarded for successes.

There are some treatment programs (in my memory: Hamilton Psychiatric in Ontario, Canada, and Lake's Crossing in Nevada) that seem to have more dynamic treatment programs with more effective placements; where, even in locked wards, growth conditions are maximized, and placement development has great priority.

Max would have had a completely new set of staff to deal with each time he progressed to a lower security ward. A long list of people must take responsibility for protecting their reputations by correctly predicting future behavior. Only the mistakes of premature release make headlines; mistakes of overlong residence are less likely to be noticed.

Max was antisocial to the system and the system reacted in kind. Maybe he needed more attention, indeed certain kinds he asked for, but surely in his twenty-four years, it would be reasonable to assume he has had adequate exposure to treatment, also assuming that the treatment was there to be had.

Instead, Max adapted his disorders to the system and the system feeds his expectations. Max was rocking the boat: he wanted out but he also wanted to keep his personality intact- antisocial and all.

Was Max dangerous because of future actions or because of present attitudes? Max got the message quite clearly: conform to ward procedures and expectations, be less threatening and more humble, recognize publicly (insightfully?) his errors and rescind all blame from others.

Taking full responsibility for oneself and avoiding all displacement mechanisms would be both admirable and healthy. But Max wanted out with the personality he has. How necessary was it that he change? Another twenty-four years' worth?

Without adequate help, some of Max's colleagues should not be released. Some have, and have, repeatedly, raped or killed.

A solution is to focus our most intense resources to offer adequate help, to build on the models that appear to be working for patients treated as hopeless elsewhere.

Max had the motivation and the intelligence to begin serious deinstitutionalization work, with the right support and candor, assuming we allow ourselves to coexist with his personality and that Max's personality allowed others to coexist with him.

Max said yes, he had already changed his behavior, but no, he won't change his identity. Max will continue to gripe vehemently about life as he fights his way through it and, in some ways, he may have retained more of his health, humor, and vitality than the salaried staff surrounding him.

A paperback book I strongly recommend is *Frances Farmer: Shadowland* by William Arnold (New York: Jove Publications/McGraw-Hill, 1979) which details in moving journalistic style the incarceration and ultimate demise of a compelling screen personality through iatrogenic involuntary institutional care including a final lobotomy.

To quote Arnold's final statement: *"The first thing an investigative reporter learns about the mental health industry is that it does not like to talk about its old psychiatric cases- any old psychiatric cases. This reticence is less a frightened cover-up than a painful memory: the victims of 40 years of radical shock treatments and some 50,000 lobotomies in state mental hospitals do not make for good public relations. When I tried to confront various psychiatric authorities with the story of Frances Farmer, for the most part they simply refused to discuss it. Many of them looked sympathetic and shrugged it off as a "terrible" thing that happened a long, long time ago. They all insisted that such a thing could never happen today.*

But the sad and appalling truth is that the Frances Farmer case is not merely an isolated incident dredged up from another era. It is extraordinary only in terms of the woman's fame and great visibility (and, indeed, there are many other examples of the negative effects of radical treatment on such celebrities as Ernest Hemingway, Judy Garland, and Vivien Leigh).

The literature of psychiatric abuse chronicles thousands of more recent and equally disturbing cases-hyperactive nine-year-olds lobotomized in Mississippi, homosexuals shocked into insensibility in England, Steilacoom-like conditions in Massachusetts and Indiana and Virginia. While I was doing research in the Midwest, a Hungarian immigrant was arrested there and subjected to extensive shock therapy because he didn't speak English and his dialect had been diagnosed by a psychiatrist as the babblings of psychosis. In California, eight Stanford University researchers who had themselves admitted to a dozen different mental hospitals by pretending to be insane found they could not overcome the label "schizophrenic" no matter how normal they subsequently behaved. (They were finally released after outside intervention by the project director.) Similar stories abound.

The fact is that surprisingly little has changed in the 35 years since Frances Farmer first came under the thumb of organized psychiatry. Many states including Washington-have passed new Jaws which make involuntary commitment more difficult, but the potential for abuse remains enormous in a field where a mental patient's future may be decided on the most arbitrary and subjective grounds. Psychiatry has never been able to define precisely what is normal (or abnormal) behavior, and thus it inevitably ends up enforcing conformity to whatever the current community and government standards happen to be-whether defined by Fascist Italy, National Socialist Germany, Soviet Russia or the State of Washington.

In the past decade, the tide of public opinion has swung heavily against traditional psychiatry. Recent research indicates that schizophrenia is attributable to an excess of receptors in the brain for a chemical messenger called dopamine, a condition which is probably related to heredity and nutrition. And this could conceivably make much of the practice of psychiatry obsolete. Laing, Szasz, and other radical therapists are still gunning away at their colleagues, and virtually every theory and treatment has been challenged by one eminent psychiatrist or another. An increasing number of studies made by psychiatry itself, in fact, confirms that suspicion that mental patients often get well faster when given no treatment than when given conventional psychiatric therapy.

And yet, despite this landslide of damning evidence and new information, institutional psychiatry has still managed to hang on to its extra-legal power and medieval treatments. Psychiatric associations have battled off attempts to outlaw shock therapy in numerous states. The big pharmaceutical companies continue recklessly to market the maze of mind controlling drugs before their side effects are thoroughly known. The population of the 337 public mental institutions-including Western State Hospital at Steilacoom-has swelled to nearly four times the prison population, and in the past decade more Americans died in mental hospitals than died in battle in all wars except World War II.

Even more ominous is the fact that, after a 15-year fallow period in which psychosurgery fell from fashion; it is now undergoing a worldwide resurgence. Various subtle and almost undetectable operations with names like "hypothalamotomy" and "amygdalotomy"-operations which, largely, grew out of the Freeman transorbital experiments of the late '40s-have been developed and widely performed in the '70s. According to some estimates, nearly 1,000 lobotomies a year take place and as the procedures become more simple and refined, the possibility of their use by a totalitarian government as a means of mass mind control becomes chillingly plausible.

The mentality of the system which deals with supposedly abnormal behavior is virtually unchanged since the 1940s. The chance of an individual like Frances Farmer being trapped and destroyed by this system is as real today as it was then. The bitter legacy of her story is not that such a fate could strike a public figure protected by the privileges of celebrity, but that it can happen to anyone."

(Arnold 1955, 2017).

This concludes the excerpts from "Max on Max" in the 2005 *Iatrogenic Handbook*.

Max Revisited

The real name for Max is Ray Ward. I used a pseudonym in my chapter printing his words because he was still in the maximum security ward of a Colorado State mental hospital. I didn't want his candor punished or worse. Ray understood this but wished someday he could get credit for his narrative. This is that day.

Among many things Ray was right about in his narrative, his assertion that behavior outside was often different than behavior inside was born out by dissertation research by Al Roske in his 1984 doctoral dissertation on predicting violence.

Ray found a pro bono attorney who took on his case. No small feat for either of them

Ray was called "JC" by the inmates in his ward as he was continually sacrificing himself to represent their needs or complaints. As he said, he was shackled often. But locksmith that he was, he still released himself to walk by the guards to go to the bathroom and smirked on the way back as he re-shackled himself. Not amusing to the guards.

He feared not much on the inside but was really anxious about adjusting to the outside. And still he wanted the chance. So he wrote me to ask for my help.

I had visited the maximum security ward once before and met him the first time there. The inmates were all lined up in a bunch, Ray in front. Ray looked like a young cowboy and smiled a lot.

I was there to meet and face down a serial killer who I had learned was supposed to kill me on his next weekend pass (another story). I had already made the hospital administrator cancel weekend passes for maximum security inmates. Killers and rapists should not get rewarded for good behavior by free access to new victims. Still, my intervention was not popular with these inmates. Understandably. They looked tense.

Ray stood with eleven other inmates but I knew there should have been one more.

I asked about the one I had come to see. Ray smiled and said *"Oh, he's hiding behind me."* An ugly head peered over Ray's shoulder and then hid back out of sight.

It was that night, back at home, that I recalled that my psychology intern way back in the 1970s told me of an earlier meeting with Ray then in his prison years. Ray had just killed his attacker and was facing the possibility of his execution. My intern, the now distinguished retired NIMH psychologist Roland Garcia, recalled that it had been his job to test Ray. Both were alone in a room for that purpose. Roland said he looked into Ray's *"cold blue eyes"* and they both knew that one more murder might make no difference in the penalty.

But Ray cooperated and consequently he was sent to Maximum Security in the state mental hospital rather than be executed.

Ray thought I was the right person to ask and, once I read his letter, we began a correspondence. One letter he smuggled out through his lawyer had his narrative which, with his permission, I published in my *Iatrogenics Handbook*. Then he had his lawyer contact me.

That was faster. I sent the lawyer a psychological diagnostic test to give to Ray under professional conditions. The computer scoring supported my impressions. Ray was sane and did not belong in a mental hospital's maximum security ward. He did have a personality diagnosis but we all knew of his insistence on candor over diplomacy which fit the diagnosis perfectly. The lawyer presented the computerized results to a judge and Ray was ordered conditionally released in three months, absent any violent episodes in that time.

That really tested Ray Ward. Staff and a few inmates all provoked him, hoping to spoil his exit. I kept in touch with him, gave him my California address, promising I would see him on the outside if he kept himself incident-free. And he did.

The test evidence allowed the lawyer to prevail. Ray was released at last.

Staff and patients had a betting pool on how many days he would be free before he was arrested and returned. Nobody ever collected.

But release was conditional first for a year in the custody of his distant relatives in Missouri (always pronounced *"Misery"* by Ray thereafter without any trace of humor). In a way it was a perfect transition. His days were all carefully constrained and constant. He worked with them on a farm from dawn to dusk, interrupted only by meals and a set bedtime. Sunday was the exception and that was church.

They spoke very little to Ray. His days were always the same so the time passed quickly.

His only error was occasionally using curse words at meals but not in anger, just habit: *"Pass the frigging salt please"*.

When his year was up he got on a bus and headed for my home in Fresno, California.

I opened the door one sunny day and there he was. After meeting my two daughters, now high school age, and a good meal, he slept on my couch that night.

I cannot recommend this home-centered approach to any therapist. Breaks all the rules.

Sometimes though you have to listen to that whisper in your ear saying that this moment is different.

Nine times out of ten it might have been disastrous. I trusted that this was the tenth.

It was.

Not before he promised me that he would take his anti-epilepsy meds and never drink alcohol again (which with the meds precipitated his probability of arrest and return to max.) He kept his word.

I should have asked for one more thing.

In the morning, I got him to social services. They placed him in a dingy group bedroom with five other men while overcharging each of them more than enough for a penthouse condo. Ray was resourceful about this. He married his social worker. Shelter and food secure.

Ray now spent his days working as an upholsterer. His spare time was invested in coaching troubled boys of which Fresno had ample supply. Ray was great at this and soon he was much loved in that community. His only vice was heavy smoking.

I thought addressing that might be too much at once. So I let it slide. The years rolled by. When my youngest daughter graduated from UCLA in theater, Ray, along with hypnotist Len Elkind, became the chaperones for her party. One guest said Elkind looked like Dr. Strange, but who was the cowboy with him? These two security chaperones were loudly appreciated. When I married my wife Becky in 1994, Ray was an honored guest. More years gone by.

In time we talked on the phone as I then lived hours away from Fresno.

In a last conversation he confided that he had lost the use of his lungs and was now breathing only with the help of a heavy device that kept him bed bound and alone. I promised I would visit in two more week ends.

When the time came, I called ahead.

A nurse said he had been a most wonderful man but had died the week before. His lungs just gave up.

Everybody missed him.

That includes me. Still.

An Honorary Catholic

Optional Theme: *Another Brick in the Wall* (Pink Floyd) https://www.youtube.com/watch?v=5IpYOF4Hi6Q&ab_channel=Piccologollum

I taught at St Bonaventure University (SBU) from 1967-1969. I left there for a job in Canada as soon as possible after Dr. M.L. King's assassination in 1968.

But while still there at SBU, I became a young president of the local AAUP, a union job nobody else on the faculty really wanted.

(My celebrated uncle Manny Fried, who once stood up to senator McCarthy's 'House Un-American Activities Committee or HUAC, would, I thought, be proud of me at only age 26 for this. When I told him about my leadership with the AAUP, his measured comment was *"Bunch of pussies"*. Decades later when we were much closer, and he had resumed his movie and stage acting career, he couldn't recall ever saying that and said he respected my union work there, but he was being honest both times.)

Because of my AAUP role, I was invited by the admin and the hosting English department faculty to come to an after party for a visiting poet, one Allen Ginsberg.

Allen had already earned fame as a Beat poet and as one of Kerouac's group. But to SBU admin, he was more noted for being a homosexual,

Jewish, and especially for his last public reading in which he had dropped his pants for emphasis. Even in the late freedom oriented 1960s, this was a lot for the Franciscan Catholic university.

When Allen actually did his reading there, audible gasps occurred frequently from many priests and nuns whenever his hand moved anywhere near his belt but no unveiling happened that time.

At the after party, Ginsberg was surrounded by English faculty who, for at least an hour, surrounded him with nonstop conversation. Never once in that hour did I see him get an opportunity to speak. Apparently these faculty were more interested in impressing him than in getting to know him.

Finally I walked through the crowd to him in his hostage chair, leaned over, and quietly asked him if he had been given anything to eat yet, He looked up, smiled, and whispered *"No! Rescue me!"*

I just announced that our guest would be going for a walk with me and we would be back soon. Allen stopped briefly in the kitchen where his partner was trying to forage and let him know we would be back soon.

Once sitting in a nearby diner, quiet reigning at last, I asked him about his visit to St Bonaventure University, known for Franciscan kindness and hospitality.

Between bites, he said his interest in coming was to visit our library archives, an important source for a book he wanted to write.

But that afternoon, on arrival at our library, the librarian priests refused to give him access, swearing at him profusely. According to

Ginsberg, their hostile verbage was the worst he had ever heard, including hateful phrases well worth pondering.

I told him I was glad to hear there was something superlative about his experience at our Catholic university and, possibly, these new words and phrases he admired might then be the basis for another book. He shrugged but smiled. Another great idea bypassed eventually by life's passage.

As to the era, my union role allowed me to become friends with Father Jerome, the Vice President for Academic Affairs. He was a gentle well-read elder statesman, wise and kind. His attempts to convert me were interesting but unfruitful, yet still we remained friends.

As we were walking across campus, a young woman walked by with the word "**FUCK**" in lipstick red on her forehead. Jerome looked to me and nodded sadly at how life had grown to be so full of this suffering for him, the accelerated decline of civil discourse as he gently experienced it.

I waited for him outside as he entered an auditorium to do a brief introduction. Ten minutes later he was back but without his clerical coat. When I asked him about it, he just resignedly said it had been stolen while he was speaking.

On the other hand, women had just been admitted as students in the university. They had a 10 PM curfew and their women-only dormitory was padlocked every night until morning daylight.

One of my students for her class project surveyed the coeds on their sexual practices. She discovered a bi-modal distribution in which about half stated they were celibate while the other half claimed so much sexual experience that not even the dorm's pet kittens or parakeets were safe.

This senior class presentation drew so much attention that our classroom had to be moved to the auditorium to accommodate interest.

The student presenter began her talk with a brief pornographic film excerpt, followed by some comment on the exploitation of women.

After all of this, I sought out Father Jerome. Only the week before, a professor at Notre Dame had been fired for showing such a film in class.

Jerome reassured me, not for the first time, that he and his peers accepted psychologists as a necessary evil, a cross between physicians and perverts.

I also agreed with him that I would volunteer to debate birth control with a very devout biology professor in our auditorium.

Again a full house but this time mostly priests, seminarians, and nuns. After the usual arguments from both sides, I asked the males in the audience to please stand if they had never been sexually attracted to an available woman. Nobody stood up (gay priests stayed secret in those days). I then asked them to stand if they had actually had sex with every one of these women. Again nobody rose. I wondered out loud: how many unborn children had been aborted by this abstinence? To my surprise, some applause and a few cheers.

(In my work there as a therapist, I soon learned that few priests there for counseling had prioritized their vow of abstinence by abstaining from complying with their vows of abstinence.)

A final memory. SBU was mostly a white male rural Catholic university. The exception was recruitment for their national championship basketball team. For this, recruiters scoured the black community in east Buffalo, New York.

Thereby recruiting a few very large athletic black male students who were also straight A students. These few black males were the first such students the white majority ever had known. As such, the white students generalized, an important basis for prejudice, and assumed these Olympian ebony athletes were typical of their race. The fear to compete with anybody of color was prevalent as I recall that Bert Karon had often found as a main basis for white racism. Much the same for the Neo-Nazis in America who even now chant *"They will not replace us"* about Jews.

(I do remember student Bob Lanier, eventual pro NBA center, crammed into my car and commenting on how amused he was by this.)

My department chair was a very fine person and psychologist. He was also a priest. As such, he was ordered by his Bishop at the beginning of Fall classes to move to New York and staff the diocese there. Many of their priests were dropping out and the Bishop thought a good psychologist might stem the flow.

(Actually that psychologist in time became convinced of the wisdom of his patients and dropped out himself to marry a nun who had dropped out with him.)

This meant I took his place to run his counseling psychology course for seminarians.

So it was I taught my only course for students about to become ordained priests, one entitled Pastoral Psychology.

Once again I noted the emphasis on obedience that the church militant had demanded of my department Chair now was manifested in my seminary students. When, in the first class meeting, I asked them for their own ideas on what would be useful to learn about psychological counseling, I was told that their Bishop had ordered them to learn and obey whatever I chose to do as the teacher.

Hmm. I asked them to consider how they would respond if a little girl, one who had benefited from their counseling, gave them a flower in thanks. Many said they would not accept that or any other gift- they were doing counseling for Christ, not for their self or for the girl. Others said they would take the flower and say thank you, identifying their primary client as the girl.

I confirmed once again that they were all bound to do as I ordered while in this class. Affirmed.

At the close of my class meeting, I ordered them not to come to the second class or any other of my classes unless they genuinely wanted to learn about counseling. About helping the people who came to them for help. Enough to accept the flower with thanks.

Next week only a little less than half the class arrived. The ones who would spurn the girl's flower were gone.

Now I had a great Pastoral Psychology class. Also the last one I would be asked to teach there.

Years later the followup was gratifying. The best students became very helpful priests.

I still wonder about the ones who never came back to class. What were *they* like as priests?

A Mixed Method for Pattern Emergence (MMPE)

Optional Theme: *Tumbling tumbleweeds* (Marty Robbins)
https://www.youtube.com/watch?v=EvgMAaqSg3o&ab_channel=MartyRobbins-Topic

Nonconforming "Bad Data"

It was 1958. I was in my first year as an applied physics major in an engineering college. We had a research lab that allowed us to individually replicate basic experiments. Once done, each of us would plot the data points to see how close they conformed to the expected curve, one historically described by a mathematical model.

Any data point not falling on the expected curve we were to circle and write "bad data" above it. The assumption was that these outliers were artefacts, simply errors in our procedure. The fewer the outliers, the higher the grade. That such nonconforming data might tell us something new of value was not being taught.

A few years later, as a psychology major in a university, I learned from some very progressive young faculty that discounting unexpected data points would be considered bad faith. The curve followed the actual outcomes and that was that. I enjoyed the freedom of this honesty. Much later the focus on complete honesty became this key aspect of Chaos Theory: the rigorous inclusion of all the exact research results, anomalous appearing or not, fitting the research theory or not, to each and every decimal point (Butz 1997, Butz & Schwinn 2004).

In my decades with international psychologists, I have been impressed by how often the most pioneering and distinguished leaders in their country readily migrate to the international associations. While the numbers are not always overwhelming, the company always is. Here the future of our field incubates. Those open to learning from unexpected research results lead the way.

A Mixed Method for Pattern Emergence (MMPE) and its Quantum future

In a special pair of reports on quantitative and qualitative research standards in the January 2018 *American Psychologist*, Levitt and friends contributed a major advance to APA style and its future companion *Publication Manual*. In a long awaited inclusion of qualitative methods, it added recognition for valid blending of quantitative and qualitative mixed methods, capturing a longstanding reality.

As comprehensive and helpful as this overdue step was, the article's very brief *"recommendations and future considerations"* section might have upgraded to contemporary computer age technology options, even including actual quantum computing (Bar-Ilan University, 2018; Shaked *et al*, 2018).

Having supervised more than 125 psychology doctoral research dissertations for nearly five decades, it was easily noted that in the evolution of research methodology, recognition always trailed practice.

In the 1970s, quantitative method was the respected approach although qualitative methodology was already successfully being used.

In 1972, a highly respected and very progressive community psychologist was sent to our psychology doctoral program in California to advise us on our application for APA accreditation. George haphazardly (he said randomly) chose ten doctoral dissertations from our library, taking them to a private room for review.

In only a very few minutes he emerged, concluding that we needed to radically improve our dissertation research.

He acknowledged that they seemed creative, comprehensive, and tackled important topics. But, he stressed, only two of the ten used analysis of variance (AOV). At that time, he stated, more than 80% of articles published in APA journals used AOV rather than 'lesser' quantitative approaches.

Would not a better approach be to match the analysis methods to the research question being asked? No, he smiled benignly, kindly lecturing us on the culture of scientific acceptance and its expectation of conformity. He particularly urged future avoidance of *any* qualitative approaches.

Our professional school president immediately revised a required course on quantitative methods to emphasize AOV.

In subsequent years, in both university departments of psychology and in free standing professional schools of psychology, the divide between quantitative and qualitative analysis, between the numbers people and the word-pattern people, continued.

Professional school graduate students often were allergic to those Arabic symbols called numbers. Although it was useful to occasionally point to the utility of numbers in things like their paycheck. (An instructor tried teaching statistics with hypnosis to avoid this trauma. It didn't work, but she was very popular for trying.)

Psychology department faculty, on the other hand, avoided qualitative approaches at all costs. One Canadian university department blocked most clinical graduate students from degree completion by requiring the passing of a quantitative statistics class that few PhDs would survive.

Yet later decades saw mixed models using both approaches increasingly appear in both professional school and department dissertations. In this 21st century, they have become common and, more to the point, effectively address the research question being asked.

That the January 2018 *American Psychologist* printed two separate reports on modern standards, one quantitative and one qualitative, demonstrates that the old divide perpetuates.

Still, in including mixed models in the qualitative standards, academic acknowledgment of a longstanding research reality took a major step forward.

How about another step then for *"future considerations"*, one consistent with today's reality and potential?

Modern quantum age computer programs could now sift through voluminous mountains of mixed method data on a global scale.

For example, let's call it a *"Mixed Method for Pattern Emergence"* (MMPE) approach.

This could selectively investigate unexpected data patterns with an integrated analysis, a method of following extraneous outcomes to discover the most valid useful ones.

The Five Key Elements of MMPE

<u>Efficiency Percentages</u> (Morgan 1968). What percentage of the sample participants are accurately described by a statistically significant outcome? A goal of approaching 100% accuracy melts away emergent patterns of statistical significance that still fail to describe many or most sample participants.

<u>Multiple Causality.</u> Beginning with the breadth of individual differences, computerized analysis will immediately develop patterns for every substantially important bimodal or multimodal context variable (age, time, region, gender, health, economic, antecedent conditions, etc.) proving a more complex but effectively valid picture. There is rarely only one truly important finding. Let's get them all.

<u>Replication</u>. Two or more independent but comparable samples of extensive data focused on the same variable. More replications means more predictive stability. A classic approach rarely to be found in time-limited cross-sectional doctoral and grant-funded research.

<u>A Central Portal for International Data</u>. The plan for a national central patient portal has foundered in the United States although advocates remain strong (Segal 2016). Input on a global scale would be more powerful, possibly more likely, yielding mountains of key information in a variety of essential categories. With MMPE, epidemiologists quickly locate causes, cures, and prevention factors for disease. Psychologists will have no shortage of essential questions to ask. And be answered. Let's say trauma (Morgan 2012) or even

cancer. These data would flow from an international expansion of central portal practitioner qualitative or mixed case data, failures as well as successes.

Enhanced Analytic Speed. All computers are fundamentally quantitative. Sifting through numerical context, they can seek and find usefully valid qualitative patterned solutions. And fast. We already have modern computer programs available for a more rapid pattern analysis of quantitative and mixed model data (Woolf, N.H. & Silver, C., 2018).

Now, moving into actual quantum computing, we can foresee near instant pattern emergence solutions from huge international samples that can be applied to our most pressing problems.

The very nature of quantum computers stemmed from investigating those anomalous data points in quantum research. That it works at all, much less so impressively, demonstrates a future available by following the path of nonconforming "bad data".

This five-element international MMPE approach is an opportunity to substantially upgrade our consideration of the "recommendations and future considerations" of these research procedures or standards.

Back to that Engineering College

In all fairness, one of my professors was actually quite meticulous, at least in his evaluation of us students. He felt the traditional grading system was insufficient to fully express exact levels of student inadequacy.

So he remedied this by expanding the F (failure) part of the ABCDF scale to 1F 2F 3F 4F or 5F. Assignments were graded accordingly. In his system, the 1F would then be the median grade.

One day he was demonstrating how to take a figure on paper and draw it on the blackboard with three dimensions such that it could be readily built. He challenged me to leave class and bring him a picture of anything so he could demonstrate his ability, knowing that we would then of course each accumulate more levels of F in trying to follow his example.

But I had already been reading about psychology, my next major, and found just the picture to hand him for his demonstration. It was an Escher-style perceptual illusion, not one to be built in our three dimensional world. Nor, despite many tries, was he able to draw it for construction that day.

Despite his extensive negative grading system, of which I certainly had consistently achieved data points in the lower half, he surprised me at the end of the semester by giving me a passing grade.

When I asked him why, he simply said he didn't want to see me repeating his class. Or, for that matter, ever see me again.

There were in fact some dedicated and excellent faculty there. Even the Swiss economics professor whose saliva made our class retreat entirely to the drier back rows.

But I had chosen physics at this college so as to explore with experts as to what was known about the secrets of the universe. Instead we were charged with learning about the secrets of plumbing and refrigerator repair.

Their motto was: *"The workman that needeth not to be ashamed"*.

To avoid that shame I planned another path.

Combing through descriptions of other majors, I realized that my main career goal was actualizing the best promise found in science fiction. It appeared as though the psychology career was closer to this.

Sixty years later, looking back, that certainly was to be the case. Even moreso in this 21st century.

So for my third year of college, I transferred to a large university to join the ranks of psychology students, a field I fit much better immediately. A move I never regretted.

Where all honest research results were understood to be worth understanding, expected or not. *Especially* if not.

Where to from here?

We can now search for solutions to the most pressing challenges to our human family, including those causes, cures, and prevention of disease.

Is this science fiction? Not so. Not anymore.

Are we ready?

The Naked Latvian

Optional Theme: *You can leave your hat on* (Randy Newman)
https://www.youtube.com/watch?v=C99ZPoKkGmg&ab_channel=RandyNewman-Topic

"Results! Why I have gotten a lot of results. I know several thousand things that won't work." -Thomas Edison, 1930.

"You can tell a poacher by how he orders his eggs." –Uncas Slattery, 2000.

We ask psychological assessment tools to guide us in the three aspects of description, prediction, and communication. We ask of evaluation much more. The longer we have been in the field, the more experiences come to mind, a regular buffet of associations. Here are a few.

Personnel Selection

While a visiting professor in Canada, I was asked by a local bank president to assist him in a personnel transition situation. I agreed to develop a battery of computer scored tests that might add a dimension of understanding to the administrators being evaluated, but with the caveat that an actually hiring or promotion decision should include a personal interview and actual performance data.

He asked me, as a consultant, to just do a pilot try for him with only the test results. So he submitted the responses of three administrators to me and the computer digested them, regurgitating impressive charts and graphs. I then met with the bank president and his key staff to go over the findings.

I decided to go with the most uncomfortable one first. "This person's results suggest a person who is highly likely to depart from accepted ethical practice and would be a hiring risk" was my kindest interpretation of the sociopathic pattern on the charts. The president grinned widely and everybody looked relieved. "Yes" he said "we had him take this test just before we fired him and had him arrested for embezzlement. I told you this testing was the way to go. Why, look at how much trouble we would have saved if we had known this early on!"

So this was a test of the test. Hmmm. I moved on to the second set of results. "This person is a highly creative and intelligent individual that should be highly successful at whatever he undertakes" I said, hoping it was not another felon. "Right again!" said the president and all grinned, especially the highly successful vice president who had taken the test and was sitting right there in the group.

At that point I had a feeling I should quit while I was ahead (or "Quit while you are behind" as my youngest daughter liked to say). The probability of a third and final success seemed remote, particularly now that it was clear that all three sets of results were already well-known employees.

But, following many caveats again, I was ready to move to the last of the three protocols, an apparently straightforward one. "This person is normal in all respects, stable and reliable. His only low scores are in creativity and independent thinking. As long as ideas come from others and the situation is well structured, he would do well, possibly in accounting or maintenance." Following a long silence, the president said "Well, I suppose that is about right. Thank you professor." Of course, the third set of results was from that president.

My departure was cordial enough, all things considered. It was Canada after all.

I was not invited back.

Preconceptions

While still there in Canada, my colleague Don Marum and I were called in to consult with the regional hospital's psychiatric staff. The affable chief psychiatrist (it happens) took us to the only locked ward.

There were a variety of developmentally disabled adults engaged in various desultory activities. The Chief took us to the far corner where an immense naked man sat, his arms folded and his lips in a pout. He probably held the weight of two men and reminded us of how close we humans are to primates as he sat there in pink skinned obesity and hairy belligerence.

We were told that he was from Latvia and spoke very little English but was assumed to be of very low intelligence. Because of his size, staff was reluctant to force him to keep his clothes on and had turned to us.

Dr. Marum immediately noted that the patient must have a huge appetite. He suggested that he be put on a behavioral reinforcement regime where he would be fed a treat for every article of clothing he put on.

While the Chief was mulling this over, I asked him "Why do you think he doesn't want to put his clothes on?"

Marum and the Chief seemed to think this question was not helpful and ignored it, so I asked a more specific one: "*When* does he put on his clothes?" That was easier to answer: whenever he is allowed out of the locked ward to go on a walk.

Once it was determined that he was no danger to anybody I requested that he be moved to an unlocked ward. Once this was done, the naked Latvian posed no further problems.

The Chief psychiatrist was so pleased with this outcome, he invited me back to see if we might do some evaluation research together. I chose to evaluate their use of electroshock treatment (ECT) and, to my pleasant surprise, he agreed. This was before we could prove definitively in an evidence based way with MRIs etc. that ECT was such a high risk procedure that it should never be used. (Morgan, 1999, 2004a).

As to measures, he wanted ward behavior compliance and I wanted measures of cognitive function and brain damage. Despite our different expectations and interests, we did agree in the end to use all the measures we each wanted.

And then came the research design. I wanted him to randomly choose half those who were going to get ECT and withhold it from them so we might have a control group. He vetoed that approach, saying withholding treatment would not be ethical, and wanted to assign ECT to a random group of patients who would not ordinarily get it. This I vetoed.

Clearly our expectations of what this invasive treatment would or would not do, prohibited any research. It would take modern MRIs and CAT scans to prove the issue of damage, although it still remains a psychiatric tool despite the proof.

Our ECT research was never done at that hospital but we did make a naked Latvian happier.

Validity

First I have learned to agree on the *purpose* of assessment, such as the *question* to be answered or the *mission* to be achieved. Then use the measure most likely to yield clear data that can be usefully interpreted. All else is inductive from there.

Student feedback on the effectiveness of their instruction and instructor is often littered with 10 point scales and hard to interpret questions. One might think this was a deliberate way to obfuscate the results, particularly from administrators trying to quantify impact on ordinal scales.

A simple percentage satisfaction score is probably the most interpretable (Morgan, 2005). I also very much lean toward dichotomous choices if it is a dichotomous question and, in general, brief and concise measures. The 12 point scale may *look* more valid but if it is truly a yes or no question, what in the world will three decimal points add?

Nor do the number of pages in a psychological test add to any genuine validity.

Exceptional Assessment Measures

Some test items seem somewhat strange but I suppose if the numbers show reliability and validity, being counter intuitive is fine. I am waiting though for items like: *"Sometimes I feel like none of the questions on this test have anything to do with me."* or *"When sweets are served do you feel lonely and desserted?"*

We also know that time is an important variable in testing (Morgan, 2004b). It used to be assumed, for example, that the older adults get the lower their tested intelligence scores. Even before the contemporary differentiation of fluid and crystallized intelligence, Nancy Woodruff demonstrated that removing the stopwatch from the intelligence testing procedure allowed IQ scores to increase with age rather than decrease. As we get older we get smarter but slower (Morgan & Wilson 2005).

Albert Ellis (1984) told me once that he would like every journal article that is published to be followed immediately by a rebuttal. He felt this would lead to a better evaluation of everything. Or, at the very least, a good argument.

I am tempted to include here some of the more interesting applications seen along the path, such as a brief non-invasive standardized test of human aging (Morgan 1968a, Morgan & Wilson 2004), efficiency percentages as ways to clarify assessment impact beyond statistical significance (Morgan 1968b), the most powerful genetic assessment technique to get at the roots of gender differences (Morgan 1968c), and an overlooked central tendency method for test item analysis (Morgan 1968c). (More on this in the chapter on Unopened Gifts.)

Evaluation remains the bedrock for organizational and administrative change and has brought about the empowerment and enhanced effectiveness of many an institution.

Now, the most powerful assessment study I can recall was that of the more than 3000 children deprived of public education in Virginia. Our finding, above and beyond critical periods of learning, was that tested intelligence *depends* on education; it varies with the quality of the learning environment (Green & Morgan, 1969).

The implications of this study impacted many countries even to this day- Bermuda comes to mind (Morgan & Fevens, 1981; Morgan 2004a).

But Bermuda, John Exner and the Molokai Peace Corps project, the invisible MMPI scale, and other such digressions are better left for other chapters, so I can wind this one up sooner.

My favorite offbeat assessment measure for psychologists was done by California psychologist S. Don Schultz when he held responsibility for the California State psychology license exams. It was before the current national exam.

California back then elected to score an essay exam. A major question on the essay exam, Don's favorite, asked us test takers to discuss Public Law 379 as it applied to child custody determination.

There *was* no Public Law 379 on child custody determination. The correct answer was *"There is no such law."* An acceptable answer was *"I don't know"* or *"I am not familiar with this law but in other states..."* A failing answer was to discuss it knowledgeably as though it really existed, to fake it.

This item reliably failed the few psychologists taking this test that should never practice.

I got the right answer and Don later told me he knew which paper was mine when he corrected them even though our names had morphed into numbers for the correctors.

"How did you know?" I asked. He said *"When you answered the question on how to deal with an invasive government form threatening your client's well-being and privacy by writing 'Answer abusive bureaucratic forms with bureaucratic forms of your own: send them an extensive form to fill out to justify their request', I knew it was you."* Informal days, those.

Observation versus Perception

Lightner Witmer, considered the founder of applied clinical and professional psychology, ran afoul of American professor William James, considered a co-founder of all psychology in parallel timewise with European professor Wilhem Wundt.

The issue was assessment (McReynolds 1997). James considered assessment as a form of research. So from that perspective, norms are meaningless unless procedure is held constant. Witmer preferred to follow Galton's path (Galton 1907) and vary his techniques assessing children based on individual differences, a dichotomy still at times separating researchers from practitioners. In other words, procedures were flexible depending on the child's needs.

I advocate following James when collecting data and Witmer after the data are collected. Since most intelligence tests end on cumulative failure. I usually continue with children on easier items long after those data are in so as to make the whole testing experience much less aversive. They end the experience with getting answers right, not on ending in failure.

Also in that era, we have Joseph Bell mentoring Arthur Conan Doyle when Doyle was a medical student and Bell was the Royal Surgeon. Bell's highly perceptive attention to detail and mannerisms have been considered the model for Doyle's eventual Sherlock Holmes novels (Booth, 1997). One medical demonstration attributed to Bell and passed down through medical school classes for generations was as follows: *Bell marched into the lab followed by a flock of medical residents. He turned to them and said "Diagnosis uses all your senses, Ignore any at your peril. And do not shy away from what must be done for full perception. Here is a beaker of the urine of a patient with a very specific ailment. Let us test your perception and your courage." With that, Dr. Bell dipped his finger into the urine saying, "I will now taste my finger for clues. Then it is your turn." One at a time each intern dipped their finger into the urine and tasted it. When all were done, Bell said: "If any of you had watched carefully, you would have noted that the finger I put in the urine was not the finger I put in my mouth. Do not just observe: perceive." (Farber, 1956).*

Prisoners of War

Optional Theme: *Enter the Dragon* (The Incredibly Strange Film Band) **https://www.youtube.com/watch?v=huindZPczLw&ab_channel=prlysis**

"Give a man a fish and feed him for a day. Teach a man to fish and feed him for a lifetime. Teach a man to cycle and he will realize fishing is boring."

—Desmond Tutu

It was a Sikh wedding in Chandigarh India. Two top Indian Golf pros were getting married to each other. One of them had been my student in Phoenix, Sports Psychologist Irina Brar, and we were gathering with her relatives.

A turbaned uncle was sharing his stories of close survival while at sea. As a Captain he had accumulated many of these, though he looked not much past 40. When I had a chance to talk to him alone, I suggested he write a book about his life and adventures. They were worth a read. He looked stunned, then smiled broadly. Saying "Do you understand? That is the best compliment I have ever had! I thank you for this wonderful day." I hadn't expected such a strong reaction. As the uncle joined his other adult male relatives in pushing the car holding the bride toward the groom's home (symbolizing a departure from her family to joining the groom's family; American-educated Irina said later that she would have none of this but appreciated the traditional sequence) I considered why my off-hand statement meant so much to the uncle. This strange foreign dignitary (me) had confirmed that his life events had meaning. Even in young middle age this already mattered.

In Fairbanks Alaska one of my psychology graduate students regretted her obligation to spend a supervised year in our community clinic. An Inuit, she had little to no respect for what she imagined western psychotherapy to be. She agreed to try it but reluctantly. Each of the students had their own clinical practice room to work in, one that I had them decorate with their own art and furniture, something to help them be comfortable. Something to reflect themselves and be at peace for their coming clients. My Inuit student did make her room her own in this way and began meeting community clients needing help. By the end of her year, she had changed her mind about the value of this work. "I so appreciate hearing their stories. Guiding them to the next better ones" she said. Congruent with her cultural values after all.

Here then are the true stories of two of these prisoners of war (POWs), one of them reliving it as a prisoner of long term care.

POW #1

White haired, he was older than most of the students in my Lifespan class. Maybe 60s at least. We were in Phoenix at a professional psychology school. It was that time for a volunteer to share a life-shaping event. Up until then he had been smiling but silent. Now he had an interested audience as he stepped to the front to speak.

"I was a Marine in Vietnam. But my fighting days were cut short when I was caught. I had been wounded, When I came to, I relaxed as I felt hands treating my wounds. Once I opened my eyes, I realized these were Viet Cong hands and my life was theirs now.

Why were they saving me? I soon found out.

All their own soldiers were needed to fight. So now they needed prisoners to grow the rice and other crops. That included me.

I did have a choice. If I declined to work in the rice paddies, they could execute me.

I became a rice farmer, wide straw hat and all. For some years. I lost count.

On just another sunny day, I was wading through a rice paddy when I heard voices from over a distant hill. Strange. They sounded like American words. Americans!

I could see distant figure coming over the hill. Couldn't make them out quite yet. Sun in my eyes. Then a really strange thing.

The rice around me began exploding in little bursts. Pretty like fireworks. Coming closer to where I was standing.

In what seemed like a long time but was probably a second, I realized they were shooting at me.

Now I had been rice farming there for years so my hair, blonde in those days, was long enough to reach my waist. I yanked off my straw hat and let the hair fall, raising my hands, yelling as loud as I could: "Hey! I'm an American. Don't shoot!"

The explosions stopped. I was liberated.

Back home I needed some time to readjust. For one, my wife had been told I had died in Vietnam. She had remarried and had a child with her new husband. That took some working through. I moved on.

On the better side, I got a settlement from the marines, back pay and all. And an honorable discharge. Plus the selling of my share of my former savings from the divorce I signed off on.

With new freedom and funding, I bought a big slice of land outside Phoenix. Huge. What was I supposed to do with it? I don't know. Still have it years later. Big enough for a town or village or some kind of charity. Any ideas?"

And he sat down. He then heard many ideas for his land.

So many that he told me after class it was like watching rice explode in a paddy.

POW #2

He was in a long term care facility in Greenville, California. A one story facility with a great view of forest and mountains. This was years before that beautiful northern California former gold rush town burned down completely in 2021.

As the only psychologist in that half of the county, I had to answer the call of the nurses to deal with this difficult patient.

They said he was rude, grumpy, and impossible to satisfy. He didn't want to be there and they agreed. Where else to go was not an apparent option though.

So one afternoon I went to his room for a talk. A thin and frail elder man was in his bed. I sat in a chair next to him. His roommate had been moved elsewhere so we could have privacy. That was what first helped.

He grimaced, pointing to the other now empty bed, saying *"Good riddance! I sure hope that he's not coming back!"*

"Why is that?" I asked. Opened a torrent of talk.

"Last night alone! I woke up and stepped in a pile of crap. He denied he had done it but who else was here. I can understand that he didn't make it to the bathroom in time. But, Jesus! And the food they serve here!"

"I see the connection" I said. "Circle of life. What goes in is bad enough and then when it comes out you wind up stepping in it."

He looked at me carefully and then laughed. I could see a nurse watching from across the hall, looking startled. First laugh ever from him she later confirmed.

He continued. *"You know, the truth is I've survived worse food. Though it's close. I was in a Japanese prison camp for four years. To this day I can't eat rice."*

I encouraged him to tell me about it.

"Well. I wasn't in the military but before the war, WW2, began I had a business building the best roads. Yes, the best. Asphalt is fast and cheap but they cost a lot because they just don't last. For them to be better you would have to let them dry for at least six months. No traffic. Well nobody has the patience for that. Me, as a contractor, I laid out concrete roads for the Army. They had to settle for weeks too but the US Army can make it so. And did. These roads are probably still okay, all these years later.

Anyhow, I was on Guam laying down new roads there when the Japanese invaded. Never occupied American land? Hah! They sure occupied that one. I was only a young contractor. Made no difference. I wound up at a prison camp with the soldiers. I think my tender age saved me. The food was marginal, the discipline severe. Only when the marines liberated the island years later was I freed. You know the biggest celebration in Guam even today is the anniversary of that Marine landing. Bigger than the 4th of July. I agree with that for sure!

So now I wind up back in a US Army hospital for nearly a year. But once back on my feet they give me a big surprise for my last day there.

As a contractor I was to be paid by the hour. That rate times every hour I was in captivity, 24 hours a day, was to be paid to me now by a USA government check.

That piece of paper was more money than I had ever seen or ever saw since.

I was of no mind to thank the Japanese but it sure did cheer me up at the time. It was deposited into a bank and supported me through two marriages and a lifetime that doesn't need to be described today. Eventually of course, it was all gone.

And here I am. Back where I don't want to be. With no choices.

I agreed that he was missing his choices. But I could help him find them.

We met every afternoon for two weeks. I always looked forward to his stories, learning more about concrete roads than I ever thought I would. And more.

At my much younger age than his, I had the privilege of sharing the old man's life adventures. Understanding some of the patterns of challenge to come, ones that we all face in our own way. And he was increasingly happy to tell me all of it. Said it made these adventures worth it.

The nurses were surprised to report that he had improved greatly. I had negotiated that he would have no roommate while I worked with him. Consequently he gradually warmed to the staff and they to him. So much that they would miss him now if he left.

Which was still exactly what he wanted to do. But to go where?

At his advanced age, his only living relative was a brother in Seattle who he had never liked. It was mutual, he said. He had reason and explained at length. They had never talked to each other in 60 years. But I did convince him to try.

I got the brother's address and we drafted a letter. A week later the brother responded with a letter of his own. The brother was delighted to hear from him. The past was forgotten (possibly because he was senile speculated my patient). In any case, his brother invited him to come and live with him in Seattle. They were both old now and the brother welcomed his company.

So, with great hope and the usual misgivings, my patient set out for his new home.

On his last day he thanked me for getting him out of long term care and agreed to write me a letter after a month in his new location. I gave him the stamped and addressed envelope and he was gone.

The nurses did not celebrate. He had been telling them his stories too and now they missed him. No applause for me.

A month later I got his letter. He said he was happy where he was. Better than a prison camp he said with his usual limited praise. Nor had he stepped in anything rank, he added.

Maybe from his POW years, he had learned to make sure other people left him alone.

I had learned that with patience and the passage of time, he was well worth knowing. His lifetime of stories were of value, well worth respect. He, with the passage of time, became a solid companion for his brother. They would reliably support each other through that challenging last phase of long rich lives.

Much like finally settled concrete.

And then: the Prisoner of Long Term Care

I am reminded that at that same facility and before I left, the nurses asked me to check in on a suicidal patient. I did. She had reason.

When younger she had been a nurse at that very facility, still knew some of the staff there. Had even trained some of them. Now she was too frail to go anywhere else, had no money left, and had been admitted months before. At first she was embarrassed to be a patient there. Then worse happened.

She had raised a single child by herself, a daughter. When that grown daughter had recently died in an automobile accident, she mother had not been informed of this. So she had missed her only child's funeral.

I suppose the nurses had been afraid to tell her. The omission felt like betrayal and now she would speak to nobody. Withdrawn, the staff feared she was a suicide risk.

Probably so. Her world had shrunk to a facility where she was so angry at the staff, her life's end likely may have seemed worth considering. She refused to talk about this anger or anything else with anybody. Suppressed anger is in fact a major motivation for suicide.

In a North Carolina facility, I had once seen a psychiatrist save a suicidal patient by deliberately making the patient angry at him. He insulted her until she ventilated. It worked. I always felt it was just manipulative. But it might work here.

In my approach I chose not to insult her. Not genuine and not honest. Too far from what I could justify. And no need.

I entered her room, uninvited, and sat down in a chair next to her bed. I told her I was Doctor Morgan and there to tell her the truth. She turned away from me. I reiterated all that had happened to her and said it was reasonable to be angry at the staff who knew about her daughter's death plus the funeral and never told her until it was too late. I told her I understood how sad it was for her to be a patient now where she used to be a high status nurse. She was silent when I finished for a few seconds. Then she turned in her bed and spoke for the first time that month: "*Get Out!*" she yelled. I moved on.

The nurses told me the next day that she had come around. She now could see herself collaborating with them against a common antagonist. Me. She was no longer suicidal.

Though they warned me that she had homicidal intent for me. Clearly a step up from suicide.

Attempting a further step up, I brought her a book of photographs of Venice, Italy, where she had been born. She once again yelled to me to get out and I did.

But she kept the book.

When I left the facility, the nurses continued to keep in touch.

Ventilating her anger had brought her to a new level of interaction. Amazing how just telling a life story, hurt especially, can be healing.

I had asked them to consult with her on nursing challenges and this they did. They reported that she was doing much better.

Of course, they said, her consistent request was never to see me again.

I smiled and complied.

Cleanliness in the Intensive Care Unit

Optional Theme: Sweet Nothings (Brenda Lee)
https://www.youtube.com/watch?v=bSv4YfF-E-M&ab_channel=cwinter7

Friday night. The ambulance took 8 hours to arrive.

Once inside though, they did deposit me quickly at the hospital. My surgeon had been waiting but left, saying he would operate in the morning. Instead, I was rushed to the Intensive Care Unit (ICU) where five nurses waited for me in a large friendly room.

Flashback to my Christmas stay 20 years ago in the Stanford Hospital ICU. They had all the hallways and room art blocked so as to wrap them each like Christmas presents. I was brought in to share a room with another patient. He was a 400-pound man who had been constipated for a week. As I got settled in my own bed, he was completing his own first successful enema. Unforgettable.

But this Albuquerque ICU was to be different. The one male nurse stepped forward and said, to protect the unit from outside bacteria, I needed to be sanitized right away. I was ordered, in friendly tone, to strip and lie on the bed. Nobody else agreed to do the same, but I complied.

While the female nurses watched, the male one anointed me head to toe with antiseptic.

Still, the shortest nurse, a Nepali woman, pointed out that the male had omitted anointing my genitals. She decided to step in and fix that omission, taking a full 15 minutes to leisurely bathe and massage my genitalia in some soapy substance while the others took note.

Before I was discharged days later, the ICU non-medical administrator, Chris Gonzalez, asked me if anything had stood out during my stay in his unit. So I shared this first cleansing experience from the night I had arrived.

I could tell he was reading this as a complaint. Not so.

I smiled and added: *"No, Chris! That was the best hospital welcome I ever had."*

It was.

Fire that Lasts

Optional Theme: *Amazing Grace* (Soweto Gospel Choir) https://www.youtube.com/watch?v=ZoJz2SANTyo&ab_channel=ScutterMartin

Some fires can last a lifetime. They live on as burns that can be inside as much as outside. They may never heal. Call it PTSD or early childhood trauma. For victims, families, responders, survivors. It calls for very special care.

Mid-morning on March 1954 in Buffalo New York's Cheektowaga. (The original Iroquois Seneca name was kept in honor of those from whom the land was stolen.) Still winter with towering snow drifts, many black from steel mill pollution. Around my school, the snow was still white. A pristine seasonal portrait. Except for the pillar of smoke coming from behind the school.

I was marching outside with my eighth grade class on the way to an emergency assembly in the auditorium for the whole school. I asked a teacher marching with us what the unscheduled assembly was about. She said nothing and was crying. A very bad sign.

A pillar of smoke rises from the roof of the annex shortly after fire broke out . . . flames were just beginning to break through.

The school principal had a solid hold on his job. For years he had come in within or under budget, even when the budget was inadequate for the educational or safety needs of his faculty and students. In other words, he protected the bottom line. He was deservedly unpopular.

As was his son John, who looked pretty much like a smaller version of his father and who was in my class. I found this to be unfair, so I befriended John whenever I could.

But his father made this far from easy. Particularly with all the lawsuits from 1954, ones based on his starring production role in the disaster.

March 1954

My classmate and friend was Ray Blendowski. He was a blond-haired athletic boy, very popular with the high school girls.

He had a sister two years younger, Patty, who had an incredibly loving spirit. She seemed wise beyond her age and, to her downfall, spent her days being sure to take care of everybody else.

One day, when I was visiting with Ray, she whispered that she was going to marry me when we were old enough. I didn't laugh. Strangely enough that seemed to me like a very good idea, even though I was only 13 and not ready to think seriously about such things.

After graduation, Ray would join the Marines. Eventually he would do what the majority of New York state people do when they tire of cold weather. They move south to Florida. The few going west to California instead usually claimed that to be the happier choice. Ray though died in Melbourne, Florida, in 2002.

Back to the morning of our march to the auditorium assembly.

Behind the school were temporary wooden structures from the decade before. Eight classroom wooden annexes were added onto the existing brick school building to accommodate the influx of new students resulting from the 'Baby Boom' following WWII.

The principal decisively kept them on as supplemental classrooms past their prime, thus saving money in the school budget.

Since Buffalo remained in winter throughout the school year, a primitive boiler kept each of them warm. Somewhat. According to newspaper reports, the boiler had previously emitted gas fumes and was known to be faulty. The glass window panes were small and old. The windows themselves were too stuck to open. Each wood annex building was a fire trap. But it saved money. The principal kept them as they were.

That morning of March 31st a sixth grade music class was in session in one of these annexes.

There and then the boiler exploded.

Next to the only door, the flames covered the exit instantly. Survivors said they had no more than a minute to get out.

I was told that a visiting salesman took immediate action before anybody else, smashing a small window pane with a chair and leaping through. Saving himself.

The windows were all still stuck closed. So a student followed the salesman's example but with a lower pane and squeezed through, cutting himself with the glass. The two teachers broke window panes then, going through as they tried to save as many as they could of the remaining 33 students. In this they succeeded, helped by a few courageous children inside in getting many of them through and out to safety outside.

Stop here. Imagine yourself in that room for that minute. You have 60 seconds to escape with your life. An explosion has covered the only door with fire and smoke is filling the room. As the fire runs across the wood ceiling, intense heat waves accelerate. The windows are stuck shut. The room is full of young children and their two teachers. You're one of the teachers. The only other adult, a salesman, has escaped by smashing a window pane with a chair and jumping through it to safety outside. By himself. For all in that room, shock stretched time. Sixty seconds seemed like much more, all was moving in slow motion. This because you have been plunged instantly into crisis mode, heart beat accelerated to its limit, adrenalin coursing through your body. Now the teachers were rising to the occasion, smashing the lowest window panes and yelling to the class to follow them. Once through, they pulled children after them, one at a time. Children ran to line up at their window, a few of the bravest helping to get the rest out and over the broken window glass. As time ran out others curled up on the floor, as far as they could get from the smoke now filling the room. They wouldn't live. It was all over in a minute. That one minute. Come back now.

Ten children were found in the ashes burned to death. Five students who had been rescued, but too late, died in the hospital from their burns for a total of 15 dead.

The teachers were hurt as well. Their heroics were magnified by those few students who stayed long enough to help others escape before them. Too long.

One boy, escaping safely, realized that his girlfriend was still inside helping other children through the window. In an instant, he forced his return to the room to join her and help. They both died in the flames.

Before they did, they helped Patty and others get out. Just ahead of Patty was little Jimmy Luongo. The teachers caught him from Patty and pulled him outside. His face hurt from the fire but he turned to help Patty out. She had waited until the last possible second. And then one more than that.

The young couple, already flashing with fire themselves, pushed Patty out. She fought to live long enough to make the ambulance with the four other fatally burned children.

Once in the auditorium, I asked the crying teacher about Patty. The teacher said that Patty had been taken to the hospital but was badly burned.

A survivor, Jimmy Luongo, later told me that Patty had saved his life but she wouldn't leave until the last child in their class was out and safe.

He said he saw her through the window when her hair was on fire like a halo. The heat had become lethal. He said this so calmly: "*Her eyes melted*".

She was one of the five that died in the hospital.

That Night

There were only three TV channels back then and the CBS Evening News with Walter Cronkite was what almost everybody tuned into. This "most trusted man in America" had kept our generation's interest with such things as letting us know there was an okay maximum limit in mass produced food for rat droppings and insects. Cronkite had also shared a study where rats did better eating the ground up cardboard box than the cereal inside it. He had the freedom to say whatever he wanted to and our world listened.

That night he told the world about our school fire. The wooden obsolete classroom structures with tiny windows and dangerous heating.

The charred bodies of the children found inside. He didn't soft-pedal the tragedy.

He did stress the need for greater safety and better funding for schools. Other newscasters followed his lead.

New York State did then improve the laws on school fire safety. Thanks to Cronkite and the subsequent publicity, there began important reforms still with us today.

Post-trauma counseling, safer school construction, and fire drills became the norm for schools across America, then the world.

(Better than those earlier atomic bomb drills that had us children hide under our desks.)

But the safety of school children plus their teachers, staff, and their underfunded educational budgets are *still* with us today, seven decades later. And not just from fire.

The parents of the deceased or damaged children sued, but individually rather than as a class. Some won, some did not.

The principal somehow was described in later reports as covered in soot from the fire, inferring he had been a hero as well, though no firsthand account ever puts him in the burning room. The salesman who ran away first before any child could escape was, despite this, also described in some accounts as a hero. Somewhat overstated.

2014

CHEEKTOWAGA, N.Y. – State Senator Tim Kennedy memorialized 60 years since the Cleveland Hill School Fire in a resolution the New York State Senate adopted this week. This tragedy – which struck the Town of Cheektowaga on March 31, 1954 – claimed 15 young lives and shook the entire community. It spurred a nationwide conversation and led to important changes that have dramatically improved the safety of our schools. In the 60 years since the Cleveland Hill School Fire, no child has perished in a public school fire in New York State. Senator Kennedy called the Senate's attention to this tragic event to remember the lives lost, commemorate the heroic actions that saved hundreds of lives and reflect on the changes that have been made to make schools safer. The Cleveland Hill Union Free School District held a remembrance ceremony March 29 at the Cleveland Hill High School Auditorium, which gathered close to 800 people. It was a moving ceremony that remembered the victims of the fire and honored the heroic actions that took place that day. Senator Kennedy delivered the following remarks from the Senate floor on his resolution remembering 60 years since the Cleveland Hill School Fire.

"Thank you Mr. President. I rise today to call this chamber to recognize a tragic event that occurred 60 years ago in the Town of Cheektowaga, the Cleveland Hill School Fire. The Cleveland Hill Union Free School District will hold a remembrance ceremony to honor the victims and heroes of this tragedy this weekend on Saturday, March 29. March 31, 2014 will mark 60 years since the Cleveland Hill School Fire which claimed the lives of fifteen sixth-grade children and injured 19 others. It was one of the worst school fires in New York State history, and resulted in a nationwide reflection of school building construction requirements.

"On March 31, 1954, an undetected fire burned through the walls and tore through the corridor of the wood-framed, one-story, eight-room annex of the Cleveland Hill School, causing panic among students and faculty. With the corridor impassable, courageous teachers immediately sprang into action, directing children to break through school windows with any items available nearby. The teachers then began to lift children out of the windows, allowing most to escape to safety. Sadly, some windows were either too small to fit through or simply would not open, creating a devastating situation for the sixth grade class of Mr. Thomas Griffin, who were attending music class with Mrs. Melba Seibold. Mrs. Seibold heroically saved 24 children from the fire, and in the process endured severe burns, suffered smoke inhalation, and broke several vertebrae while jumping out the window. Tragically, fifteen children were unable to escape and perished in the blaze.

"It was a tragic day in our history, but it ultimately led to important changes that have undoubtedly saved lives. In the aftermath of the Cleveland Hill School Fire, many changes were

made to increase the safety of school buildings. There was a national movement away from wooden-framed school buildings, and today in New York State, regulations require rescue windows in classrooms to have a minimum 6-square-foot opening. Because of these changes and others, the Cleveland Hill School Fire was the last time a public school child died in a school fire in the State of New York. A clear sign that the necessary actions prompted by this tragic fire has helped keep our children safe in the decades since. Thank you." https://www.nysenate.gov/newsroom/video/timothy-m-kennedy/senator-kennedy-honors-60-years-cleveland-hill-school-fire

Today

Jimmy Luongo was one of the lucky ones that survived the fire but with blisters and burn scars so pervasive on his face that all his elementary and high school years included continual skin grafts. I took time with Jimmy to help him see a better future. He of course was haunted by traumatic memories of that hellish minute in the burning annex. But in time he decided that he wanted to be a doctor like the ones giving him so much time to rebuild his face. It would be off to medical school then.

This day I looked him up. No, not medical school. Instead he must have decided that he wanted even more to be like those heroic teachers that had saved him and so many other children. He dedicated his life, decades more, to being a teacher like them. And his face had healed.

LUONGO - James L.

October 10, 2019 of Cheektowaga at age 76. Beloved son of the late James J. and Leonore (nee Boats) Luongo; dear friend of Jack Gaglia, Denise Rosten, the Armone family and the Koutsandreas family. Jim was an elementary school teacher with Maryvale Schools for 33 years. No prior visitation. A Mass of Christian Burial will be celebrated on Thursday at 10:00 AM at Infant of Prague Church, 921 Cleveland Dr., Cheektowaga. Entombment to follow at Holy Sepulchre Cemetery. Arrangements by AMIGONE FUNERAL HOME, INC.

Tonight

In that twilight time just before we drift into deep sleep, we can ask a question that matters to us. The answer can be there for us when we wake up in the morning.

This method is from the Dean of Clinical Hypnosis, David Cheek, who taught us to use our deep delta sleep to come up with the best answers to our most pressing questions.

Like now:

Where is Patty to be found? Jimmy? The other lost children?

What *is* now?

I woke up knowing that Patty and the other children remain alive and well in their own all-too-brief time of existence. At the end of that short time, their being with us was over.

We access that place in our past where they still live with the key of memory, memory that we use to honor their statues in time.

As I recall from my own experience years later (see the Day of the Hobbit chapter), there was no pain after the moment of death. None. No matter the transition.

Just a peaceful floating above the ground in a safe and beautiful place. For me, it was a sunny garden with tall green grass. You feel that you can go anywhere. But you are happy right where you are. So you stay for the long moment.

Time is a place.

Patty and all the rest will always live in that place. An eternal time statue to grace.

We won't forget.

Closing Optional Theme: *Sleepwalk* (Santo and Johnny) https://www.youtube.com/watch?v=YBRCvVpknvg&ab_channel=OfficialMusicHome

Three Weddings

In my time in San Diego, 1979, an extraordinary psychiatrist friend had begun an intentional community for patients diagnosed with schizophrenia. No medication, ECT, or any other invasive high risk interventions. Just therapeutic community. It had been very successful for a year when she asked me to consult. Intrigued, I went to meet with her patient group. Nobody was to be hired for the program without their consent. My interview with them was short and direct. I was asked just one question: "What about you gets you in the most trouble?" I answered "My sense of humor". They caucused. Finally their spokesman stood up and said "That's true for us too. We want to hire you." Deal.

The early 1970s in San Francisco.

The war in Vietnam was still on, extended by Richard Nixon. Those choosing to avoid being drafted to continue the invasion, found creative attempts to dodge this possibility. One of these was to purchase a divinity degree and these were plentifully available.

My own service obligation ended honorably in 1968 but somebody still bought me a doctor of divinity diploma from the *"Church of Universal Brotherhood"*, based in Los Angeles. It had cost $20 and was signed by a *"High Priestess"*.

So I never put this honor on a CV but still posted it in my office while I was Faculty Dean at the California School of Professional Psychology there in San Francisco.

Wedding Number One

Two of my doctoral students were due to graduate. They had planned to get married to each other at that point. Both stopped by in my office and sank together into my spacious extra-wide most comfortable guest chair.

(Years later I was asked by a former colleague if I still had that great chair. She said she loved to come by my office and sink into it as long as she could justify. When I told her I had given it away, she demanded to know why. *"People stayed too long"* I explained.)

The young couple, having noted my divinity diploma, asked me if I could officiate at their marriage ceremony. I didn't think my signature on their marriage license would be legal. But, to my surprise, the future bride had looked into this and California recognized that divinity degree as sufficient for the task. Turned out to be true.

The future groom handed me the typed script for the ceremony. They had written scripts for each of them and another briefer set for me. No thought needed on my part and I liked them both. So when my mouth opened to respond, a Yes came out.

Thorough as ever, the future bride handed me the invitation. It was to take place on Ocean Beach at Sunset the next Saturday. The very place where the famous *Burning Man* extravaganza had first begun.

And so it was.

The sunset was spectacular and the guests friendly.

We read our lines and they kissed. Cheers from guests and a few tourists stopping by.

I signed their marriage license and the event was legalized.

Whew! Seemed to be a contribution I could make.

The next day they gave me a Bonsai Tree in a small pot for my scripted service.

Wedding Number Two

I was given the opportunity as Dean to hire an assistant.

I met with the campus secretaries to see if I should be looking for any specific qualities in candidates. They were unanimous. Noting that they were all female, they really hoped I would hire a male assistant. Better gender balance for the times.

Okay. I was teaching a night class at San Francisco State University. About to graduate there with a psychology B.A. was one of my top students: an immigrant from China named Patrick. He soon was hired as my assistant back at the professional school.

Just prior to that hiring, the president of the system called me into his office for his own advice on hiring an assistant. His advice is still vivid in my memory today.

"Robert, you know I draw the line at any sex between faculty and students. These students are adults and at least as old as most of their teachers but no sex! Same as the need for no sex between therapist and patient- just not ethical! I see you nod agreement."

(Now he lowered his voice and moved closer to continue, smiling.) *"I think you may have noticed my assistant and secretaries in the outer office. Kind of attractive aren't they all? THAT is where you go for sex. Fair game. With consent of course. Any questions? Fine. Now go hire your assistant."*

The next day I hired Patrick, very much pleasing the campus secretaries. And for the next four years, the president assumed I was gay. Which he had zero approval for. I let him steam. In the last year he learned finally that I was not gay. I was told that he wondered out loud why I had hired Patrick then.

Patrick didn't stay the full time I was a dean there. But when he left for a better opportunity he asked me for a favor. He wanted to complete his citizenship initiative but would be more likely to succeed if he had an American wife. Now he had found a Japanese American woman, a very good friend, who had agreed to marry him. But just as an act of friendship and not a romantic act. Would I officiate at the marriage and sign their license?

I said that first I needed to talk privately with both bride and groom. He agreed.

In this I was assisted by Ben Tong, then my doctoral student, teaching partner, and eventual lifelong family friend. Ben and I took turns interviewing the potential bride and groom.

Patrick was grateful to his bride for this immigration help. He knew she would like the marriage to last and said he would give it a try.

Dr. Tong and I both found the volunteer bride to be really in love with Patrick and she hoped the marriage might last. We did our best to help her realize that Patrick was not emotionally there yet.

We encouraged her to postpone any wedding until they both were committed. But she saw this as her best chance to become the life-long partner she wanted to be for Patrick. She pleaded with us to go ahead.

It has been said that weddings are a triumph of hope over experience. That was her choice, she knew the risk, and so we went ahead.

The wedding was private. It seemed to go well. Ben Tong recalled: *"I never knew what ultimately became of Patrick's union with his bride. I do vividly recall their imaginative wedding ceremony. Different from conventional practice, the bride had a best man ('the best male friend in my life after my husband,' she proclaimed) and the groom had a counterpart, his best lady. Cool stuff of the '60s/'70s."*

Pat became two new things within the year that followed. He became a citizen. He became an ex-husband.

Quite likely that his ex-wife then wound up marrying her best man after all.

I decided I had done my last marriage ceremony.

Wedding Number Three

My doctor of divinity diploma was no longer on the office wall.

Despite this, a request walked into my office one day.

She was a recent graduate of the psychology school. In fact I had been Arlene's dissertation chair. I respected her ability, liked her as a new colleague, and was biased to be of assistance.

But she wanted me to perform her marriage ceremony.

In the end of a long discussion, in which I had explained fully why this was a bad idea, the very persuasive Arlene had my consent to go ahead.

This was to be just a small ceremony in her apartment's living room. She had been living there with the potential groom for a few years now with no need for a marriage. But her parents and his as well were somewhat traditional. Arlene knew they would be far less anxious about their interracial relationship if a marriage occurred. No big deal, something just for the parents comfort.

We set a date for an afternoon a month later.

A week later she happily announced that both sets of parents would be there. Hers were coming from Mexico and his from Harlem. Anticipating a crowded living room.

I gave it not much more thought until she called me one week before the marriage date.

All four parents were there. Was I going to come in for the rehearsal?

Rehearsal? Turned out that Arlene's parents were devout Roman Catholics and the groom's parents were pastors in their Harlem church.

Alarm bells.

I asked Arlene to graciously decline a rehearsal as we wanted a small family-only living room ceremony in a week. Give the parents some time to catch up on the lives of their adult children. This worked.

Life intervened. The following week was overloaded with my own work and family events. The marriage day arrived unannounced and without my adequate preparation.

I did of course have adequate anxiety. (My daughter tells me that her acting career is enhanced by a little of this. So I hoped.)

I only had a few minutes before leaving for the apartment to choose officiating materials. I took my copy of Arlene's doctoral dissertation. It was about the grandmothers who had come to the USA a century before as very young women. Leading to the birth of a very vibrant Chicano community in San Francisco. The psychology of their success against almost overwhelming odds was well worth the read.

I still needed something more. I scanned my books for something like a bible. The expectations of the traditional Christian parents required that at least. I did have a bible but it was pretty ragged looking. Instead I chose a gold-bound bible-looking volume from the shelf. Turned out it was *"A Passion in the Desert"* by Honoré de Balzac in which a lost French soldier has a romantic affair with a leopard (or lioness in some versions). Ah well, I need not actually read from this book.

Armed with Arlene's hard copy dissertation, black with gold letters on the cover, and the gold-bound French bestiality bible substitute, I arrived at the apartment.

Both sets of parents had been drinking toasts for a while. They were very welcoming in a somewhat solemn way. Impressive people. Just them, the couple to be married and me.

I stood facing the couple to be married, each flanked by their parents.

I chose to begin with honesty.

I acknowledged that I was not a priest or minister but did have legal authority to sign a marriage license and to conduct this ceremony.

I let them know how honored I was that Arlene had chosen me for this event, with the groom's consent, though my prior role had only been to Chair her excellent doctoral dissertation as she became a doctor and psychologist. I then held up that very impressive dissertation and opened it to Arlene's dedication, reading: *"La familia lo es todo para la Chicana."*

I continued: *"Or in English 'For the Chicana, Family is everything'. We are gathered here today because this young couple loves their parents. They want them to be happy with this longstanding union in a way that your parental tradition requires. So today what we do here is a celebration of love across two generations. Raising children is far from easy but it is the highest art. Art that finishes itself. As has been successful with these adult children finished and standing before you here."*

I handed the bound dissertation with its gold letters on the cover to Arlene's mother. Then opened the gold book to pronounce the young couple married. Arlene and her husband kissed.

Then all sat down. Silence. The two fathers and the groom's mother had another drink. Arlene's mother was crying.

Was this ceremony too brief or not religious enough? As is said in Singapore: trouble knocking on my door?

Arlene's mother got up and walked over to me.

She said: *"Thank you! That was very beautiful."*

I took a breath of relief. Signed the marriage license.

In a little while I left the happy family with my gold French bestiality bible tucked away in my coat pocket. Before anybody asked to see it.

That was my last time to perform a student wedding.

A service discontinued.

Alaskan Dream

Optional Theme: Cool Water (Marty Robbins) <u>https://www.youtube.com/watch?v=CvHKsrNqyO4&ab_channel=MartyRobbins-Topic</u>

An outing with Inuit in Alaska.

Sharing dreams on a cold night.

Mine was about ice fishing which I used to do as a teenager. In the dream I had a place to fish through the ice but was having no luck that night.

I could see the beautiful very large fish go by below, colorful and free.

On impulse, I pulled out my line and dropped in my sandwiches for the fish to feast on. A happy dream. The Inuit said the dream fish were them. This meant I was there to help them.

So it was.

Bonus

'WHAT DO YOU MEAN 'IT'S A BIT MUDDY'?'

Batacas

Optional Theme: *Hard to be Humble* (Willie Nelson) **https://www.youtube.com/watch?v=qdZ5wY9XxdA&ab_channel=WillieNelsonVEVO**

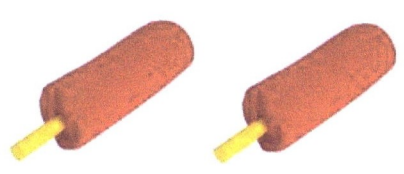

Clinical Psychologist George Bach introduced his *"Fair Fight Training"* couples therapy to our San Francisco professional school in its earliest years. By our year of 1972 it was popular with students and even a few faculty.

George began his therapy group for couples by telling them to raise their hand when they thought of something that their partner would want to know but they had been afraid to tell them.

When enough time had lapsed for group pressure to work, all hands were raised. Then George would say the group could begin: one by one each would tell their secret. Always a lively group.

George had a process for resolution. Each couple would begin negotiation by releasing pent-up hostility.

This was done by belting each other with foam rubber covered bats, ostensibly unable to damage participants. These were called Batacas.

Once exhausted or timed out, real vocal negotiations could begin. At their close, a sign of affection was expected.

One of my students brought a pair of Batacas into our classroom, explaining they were safe.

Another student was Lou Engel, a martial arts enthusiast. Lou held a Bataca high, gathered his brick-breaking Ki, and brought it down with such force that it cracked a wood desktop.

Harmless?

(After class, Lou asked me if I too pursued a discipline in the martial arts. I was hearing this term 'martial arts' for the first time, much less a required affiliation. So I just shared that I followed a non-violent path, a discipline I named Martial-Mellow. Best roasted on a non-foam stick over a fire. Followed next the generational delight of Bruce Lee movies. All was soon made clear.)

I was at the time involved in a troubled marriage, well within its final years. She eventually brought home a pair of Batacas so we could release our hostility.

Remembering Lou's demonstration, I declined. But she insisted. Now I did not want to hit her nor did I desire being hit. This I said. But she ignored this and attacked with her Bataca.

My solution in the moment was to treat this as a martial arts exercise (by then I was hooked). I would neither hit her with the Bataca nor allow her to land any hits on me.

In those, my young days, I had more speed than most. So as hard and fast as she attacked, I blocked it every time. Neither of us was ever hit. After many frustrating minutes for her, she threw her Bataca down.

I let George know that in this, my in-the-moment technique, as any psychologist might have expected, I had raised her hostility exponentially.

I also told him about Lou Engel's demonstration.

George was a good listener, highly practiced at it, but clearly was far from impressed.

Never saw Batacas again.

Or George either for that matter.

He died in Los Angeles in 1986 but no evidence that it was from Batacas.

Departures

With love for the many now departed friends including Josette Mondanaro, Tom Crowley, Bert Karon, Hans Toch, Stephen Johnson, Becky Crockett McGuane Fonda and Peter Fonda, Stuart Twemlow, Ben Camo, Nathan Hare, and my forever sister Pat Norman. Time Statue artists all. If I left anybody out, well, I wish you had waited longer.

Some of the more recent departures will be remembered here.

TIME STATUES REVISITED – BOOK ONE: ON THE JOB

Ernst Beier, Ph.D.

Optional Theme: *The Sounds of Silence* (Simon & Garfunkel)
<https://www.youtube.com/watch?v=4fWyzwo1xg0&ab_channel=SimonGarfunkelVEVO>

His life's giant contribution was about reading our silent body language.

An international psychology division for the American Psychological Association (APA), now Division 52, was originally the idea of a small group led by Ernst Beier, eventually its first President. I recall Fran Culbertson and Florence Denmark particularly among the several distinguished advocates for international involvement leading our initial charge.

We were longtime veterans of the process. I've been in APA since 1966 but I was far from the oldest in the group. I got to be the first awards coordinator, dividing the award categories between USA and non-USA recipients.

In all of this Ernst was the catalyst for progress as a leader that never seemed to tire.

His two decade age advantage over me and most of the rest of us was clearly an example of the vitality and accomplishment some psychologists keep to the end of a very long life.

Always charming and universally appreciated, Ernst epitomized what I call the Golden Rule of Proportionality: he solved far more problems than he created.

Maybe moreso than most others I have known, he was always at his best.

An international psychologist pioneer, Ernst Bier, was a celebrated expert on body language. His popular book *"People Reading"* was a best seller. His *"The Silent Language of Psychotherapy"* was a key volume for therapists.

His day job was as a psychology professor in Salt Lake City, Utah.

In the summers he would travel to exotic locales like New Guinea, following the cultural variations of body language there. He also enjoyed sailing, skiing, trekking, traveling, visiting and interviewing shamans, and piloting his own plane.

Not bad for man then in his eighties.

When I met Ernst, he looked a lot like the mustached man about town in the *Esquire* magazine.

On the other hand, he spoke with a strong German accent. Add to that his military history in World War Two, and my first erroneous impression was that he had fought on the Nazi side.

As we got to be friends, I asked him how he reconciled that experience. He seemed startled. No, he was on the *American* side.

The German accent? What accent?

In fact Ernst had been a Jewish refugee, immigrating as a young man to America and fighting as soon as he could *against* the Nazis. He had joined the US Army, Tenth Mountain Division, but was sent overseas with the 28th Infantry division. He was captured at the Battle of the Bulge by the Germans and survived a POW camp. After liberation he received the silver battle star.

Now a Jewish professor in a predominantly LDS university?

"*Exactly*!" he confirmed with a broad smile.

A few years later, he was my invited keynote speaker at a professional psychology school graduation in California.

Ernst and a restless audience waited for his turn through about an hour of preliminaries.

When I finally could introduce him, I reviewed his outstanding body language contributions briefly. Much of that was beginning to appear in television series and in books on poker tells.

I told the already restless audience that if they had read his books, they would have been able to follow his speech already. Since while he was waiting he had given it sitting there on the stage silently twice now. (Laughter.)

Now awake, they were focused. Actually, once using actual out loud spoken words, he gave a fine talk. Lots of insights graduates could use.

Still with a great German accent though.

Until suddenly he was no longer there. Or anywhere. Nobody that I asked knew.

There was a rumor that Ernst, now in his late 90s, had Alzheimers. Or, my initial favorite, that he had run off to New Guinea to be with a tribal woman.

One day I finally succeeded in tracking his phone number down and called. Frances, his wife of 65 years, answered.

Once she knew who I was, she apologized: *"I'm sorry. Ernst is bedridden now. At 99 years old, his mind is fine but he no longer can speak. You can talk to him on the telephone but he can't answer you. There's not much time. We are told he won't live out the week."*

If only I could see him. Then I knew he would answer me just fine without speech.

But I took what I could in the time we had, being thousands of miles apart.

I talked one-way for a while, reminding him of past good times, funny twists in our life, and wishing I could be there to enjoy his stories, even if by body language.

When I was done, his wife took the phone again.

She said: *"He's smiling now"*.

Pat Norman

Optional Theme: *Amazing Grace* (B. Obama) **https://www.youtube.com/watch?v=IN05jVNBs64&ab_channel=C-SPAN**

*"**Pat Norman** began her activism in California in 1971, when she founded the Lesbian Mothers' Union to address and defend child custody issues for lesbians. In 1972, she became first openly gay person hired by the San Francisco Department of Health to serve the gay community. She was a key leader in the development of AIDS care, called the San Francisco Model, which involved a collaborative network of city agencies, community organizations, hospitals,*

and healthcare providers. Norman was a lecturer and consultant to nonprofit and public agencies from 1974–1988, and was the statewide director of training for the Youth Environment Study (YES), Inc., from 1988 to 1989. She was a co-chair for the California State Mobilization for Peace, Jobs, and Justice, 1984; co-chair of the National March on Washington for Lesbian/Gay Rights, 1987; a delegate to Jesse Jackson, Democratic National Convention, 1988; a member of the Nelson Mandela Reception Committee, 1990; and a co-chair of the Stonewall 25 Organizing Committee, 1994, where demonstrators unfurled a one-mile-long, 30-foot rainbow-colored flag symbolizing lesbian and gay rights. Roughly one million participants from around the world converged on the Avenue of Americas in New York City on that day. Norman was founder, president, and chief executive officer of the Institute for Community Health Outreach, an organization that provides training for community health workers, especially focusing on underserved and stigmatized populations. She retired in 2002, and shortly thereafter moved to Kauai, Hawaii, where she lived for 20 years. Throughout the years, Norman also served on several public commissions: the Police Commission, Fire Commission, and the Human Rights Commission. She provided years of leadership on nonprofit boards such as serving as the president of the Black Coalition on AIDS, the president of SAGE (Standing Against Global Exploitation), and the president of Larkin Street Youth Center. Pat Norman was portrayed by Whoopi Goldberg in the docuseries When We Rise, which was released in early 2017." – San Francisco Bay Times, August 11, 2022

Death brings the curtain down on a life story in progress. Each of us creates our own story day to day, moment to moment. Statues in time, always there in that place, that time. Often the end is far too soon. Pat Norman's first born son, Paul, died in a car crash just as his story turned from turbulence toward a happier path with love for his wife, children, family, friends. Martin Luther King Jr had his life story ended before he ever turned 40. So much accomplished in that little time but what if he had lived at least twice as long? Such interruptions can be profoundly hurtful to those of us who had been included in that ongoing life. The more powerful their story, the greater this departure is a loss to our own. Pat Norman had the time to earn a fortunate outcome, fortunate for all the lives she touched, fortunate for the freedom and care of many generations. In San Francisco's creative non-traditional early 1970s, Pat and I heard from several sources that we had been twins in an earlier life. While this might not have been literally true, it fit us very well. From then on, we became brother and sister. Since we each periodically had been raising children on our own, now the two families came together. The children had both of us in their corner. As we got older, many of them were in our corner. It was of course somewhat of a shock to Pat's mother, Maude, when she visited and learned she had birthed a 230 pound man she didn't know about. Pat lived more than twice as long as Dr. King, like him she accomplished much for the human family as well as her own. Wish their life story had gone on at least as long as ours. Well Pat, what a story it was. Be at peace now. And hear our applause.

Hans Toch, Ph.D.

Optional Theme: *Time Keeps on Slipping/Fly Like an Eagle* (Steve Miller)**https://www.youtube.com/watch?v= 6zT4Y-QNdto&ab_channel=chinita41**

Hans Toch, an original pioneer in the fields of social psychology with emphasis on criminology and criminal justice, died June 18 2021 at his home in Albany, New York.

Born April 17, 1930 in Vienna, Austria, he escaped the ravages of the holocaust, initially to Cuba and then to the United States. He earned his B.A. at Brooklyn College in 1952 and his Ph.D. in psychology at Princeton in 1955.

He served in the U.S. Navy, and was a Fulbright Fellow in Norway, a visiting Lecturer at Harvard, and a member of the psychology department at Michigan State University before being recruited in

1967 as a founding faculty member of the School of Criminal Justice at the State University of New York at Albany, the first program in the country to confer the Ph.D. degree in criminal justice.

Professor Toch remained on the faculty at the University at Albany until his retirement in 2008, attaining the rank of Distinguished Professor and mentoring countless students and junior faculty members over the course of his lengthy tenure.

His scholarship reflected a consistent humanistic bent and a concern for representing the viewpoints, understandings, and humanity of the subjects of his writings: offenders, police officers, the incarcerated, and correctional officers.

He authored more than 30 books including such classics as *Violent Men: An Inquiry into the Psychology of Violence*; *Living in Prison: The Ecology of Survival;* and *Stress in Policing*. He received the August Vollmer Award from the American Society of Criminology in 2001, and in 2005 he was recognized with the *Prix DeGreff* award for distinction in clinical criminology by the International Society of Criminology.

He was a fellow of the American Society of Criminology and of the American Psychological Association, and in 1996 served as president of the American Association for Forensic Psychology.

Sixty years ago I was an undergraduate student in Hans Toch's classes at Michigan State University. I liked his regular two courses so much that I next enrolled with a friend in his personalized special studies research class.

Our student contributions included interviews with Malcolm X and an explorative diagnosis of the Socialist Labor Party.

Over the next decades, his own contributions revolutionized the field. A decade later in 1978, I published a debate with Bernard Diamond and others on the Insanity Defense, a book completely inspired by Hans.

By then we were longtime friends and colleagues. Turned out that we had ancestors from the same parts of Eastern Europe, so much that eventually Hans declared that we were likely related and I was his "*Homie*".

His reviews of my work that followed stood out for their clarity, brevity, and insightful humor. My favorite was the close of his cover quote for my *Iatrogenics Handbook* (2005) on the doctor's mistakes: "*If the shoe fits, it will hurt*".

He eventually said he experienced his own share of iatrogenic medical mistakes, declaring that he was at the end of his road and that his home was his hospice.

We next spent eight years still exchanging ideas, until I began to doubt his demise was likely after all, at least not in this century.

But he was bound to be right eventually. And as usual, in 2021, he was. Glad he waited at least as long as he did.

What a dear friend, gift, genius, and guide he was to me in this chaotic world. What a fine mind and unforgettable sense of humor.

He certainly loved his wife, children, and friends. It is returned.

In tribute to his brilliant sense of humor and dialogues with his students, I close

with a quote from one of my Canadian students, a nurse.

In my *Iatrogenics Handbook* (page 447) she recommended a surgery that might be applied to those lacking a sense of humor or with *Novumnotiophobia** (unrealistic fear of new ideas) or *Novumlibrophobia** (overwhelming fear of books that are new or unusual) as follows: *"The Optoectomey severs the cord connecting the eyeballs to the rectum, thus eliminating a certain negative outlook on life."*

I followed her suggestion next with the last sentence in the book: *"May we all enjoy life to its fullest, cords and balls intact."* Hans sure did.

References

Optional Theme: *Sleepwalk* (Ritchie Valens) **https://www.youtube.com/watch?v=iSIUUmFHg18&ab_channel=CassianoPastori**

Arnold, W. (1955,2017). Shadowland. San Francisco: Berkley.

Barch, A.M., Ratner, S.C., & Morgan, R.F. (1965) Extinction and latent reacquisition. *Psychonomic Science*, 3, 495-496.

Bar-Ilan University (2018) "Forging a quantum leap in quantum communication: Scientists introduce a technique that speeds up quantum information processing nearly a million times." *Science Daily*, 9 February. <www.sciencedaily.com/releases/2018/02/180209112342.htm>.

Battino, R. (2006) *Expectation: the very brief therapy book*. Norwalk, CT: Crown.

Bickford, J. (2002) *Delancey Street Foundation: American Dreams*. Las Vegas, Nevada: American Dreams.

Bloudoff-Indelicato, M. (2013) Beaver butts emit castoreum goo used for vanilla extract that the FDA regards as "natural flavoring". *National Geographic* (10).

Brandt, D. (1973). *Play Therapy with Adults: Effects on Child Rearing and Self Concept.* Ph.D. dissertation, California School of Professional Psychology, San Francisco.

Breggin, P.R. (1994) *Toxic psychiatry*. New York: St. Martins

Breggin, P.R. & Cohen, D, (2007) *Your drug may be your problem*. New York: HarperCollins.

Bütz, M.R. (1997). *Chaos and complexity: Implications for psychological theory and practice*. Washington, D.C.: Taylor & Francis.

Bütz, M.R. and Schwinn, R. (2004) "Transforming Crisis Theory in Behavioral Healthcare: Moving from Stasis to developmental adaptation." Paper presented to the Society for Chaos Theory in Psychology and the Life Sciences, Marquette University, July 16, 2004.

Cheek, D. B. (1968) *Clinical hypnotherapy*. New York: Grune & Stratton.

Cheek, D.B. (1993) *Hypnosis: the application of ideomotor techniques.* New York: Allyn & Bacon.

Cheek, D. B. & L. LeCron (1968) *Clinical hypnotherapy.* New York: Grune & Stratton Consortium for Longitudinal Studies (1983) *As the twig is bent: Lasting effects of preschool programs.* Lawrence Erlbaum: Hillsdale, New Jersey.

Davidson, A. (1999). *The Oxford Companion to Food.* Oxford University Press. p. 263.

Elkind, L. (1972) *Effects of hypnosis on the process of aging.* San Francisco, CA: California School of Professional Psychology. Unpublished doctoral dissertation.

Elkind, L. (1981) Hypnotic intervention: Elkind's contribution. Chapter 2 in R. F. Morgan *Interventions in applied gerontology.* Toronto: Kendall/Hunt, 33-58.

Elkind, L. (2017) Personal communication.

Green, R.L. & Morgan, R.F. (1969). Effects of resumed schooling on the measured intelligence of Prince Edward County's Black children. *J. Negro Educ.* 38, 147-155.

Hoehn, A.J. & Woolman, M. (1969) Operational context training in individual technical skills: ED041233. . Clearinghouse for Federal Scientific & Technical Information: Springfield, Virginia.

Karon, B.P. & VandenBos, G.R. (1981). *"Psychotherapy of Schizophrenia: Treatment of Choice."* New York: Aaronson.

Kozol, J. (1967, 1985) *Death at an Early Age: The Destruction of the Hearts and Minds of Negro Children in the Boston Public Schools.* NY: Houghton-Mifflin, Plume.

Kozol, J. (2006) *The Shame of the Nation: The Restoration of Apartheid Schooling in America.* New York: Three Rivers Press.

King, M.L. (1964, 1981) *Strength to Love.* London: Hodder & Stoddard (1964), Minneapolis, Minnesota: Augsburg Fortress (1981).

Lazar, I., Darlington, R., Murray, H., Royce, J. Snipper, A., & Ramey, C.T. (1982) Lasting effects of early education: A report from the Consortium for Longitudinal Studies. *Monographs of the Society for Research in Child Development, 47 (2/3),* 1-151.

Levitt, H. Frost, D.M.M., Bamberg, M., Creswell, J. W., Frost, D. M., Josselson, R., & Suarez—Orozco, C. (2018). Qualitative and mixed methods research standards. *American Psychologist,* 73 (1), 26-46.

Mondanaro J. (1989) *Chemically Dependent Women: Assessment and Treatment.* Lexington, Mass: Lexington Books.

Morgan, R.F. (1964a). The adaptational behavior of chicks in a spinning environment. *Psychological Record, 14,* 153-156.

Morgan, R.F. (1964b) *Uncas Slattery/ The Muddy Chuckle.* New York: Exposition. (1987 version a two-act play.)

Morgan, R.F. (1968). Need for a greater use of efficiency percentages to supplement reports of statistical Significance. *Perceptual & Motor Skills, 27,* 338.

Morgan, R.F. (1978). *Should the Insanity Defense be Abolished?* (With William Carnahan, Bernard Diamond, Eugene Turrell). National Judicial College and the Nevada Division of Mental Hygiene & Mental Retardation Proceedings, Reno: Human Services Education.

Morgan, R.F. (1982) Balloon therapy. *Canadian Psychology,* 23, 45-46.

Morgan, R.F. (1983) Community dispersion or problem resolution?: hypothetical plight of community residential patients with appendicitis. *Psychological Reports,* 53, 353-354.

Morgan, R.F. (1999). *Electroshock: the Case Against.* (With Peter Breggin, Leonard Frank, John Friedberg, Bertram Karon, Berton Roueche) Albuquerque, NM: Morgan Foundation, 1999. (Chapter IV reprinted in Brent Slife's *Taking Sides: Psychological Issues, 13th edition,* Guilford, CT: McGraw-Hill/Dushkin, 2004 and in Richard P. Halgin's *Taking Sides: Abnormal Psychology, 2nd edition,* Guilford, CT: McGraw-Hill/Dushkin, 2002. (First edition: *Electric Shock.* Toronto: IPI Publications, 1985.)

Morgan, R.F. (2005a). *Training the Time Sense: Hypnotic & Conditioning Approaches* (With Linn Cooper, Elizabeth Erickson, Milton Erickson, Gary Marshall, Christina Maslach, Paul Sacerdote, & Phillip Zimbardo.) Albuquerque, NM: Morgan Foundation.

Morgan, R.F. (2005b). *The Iatrogenics Handbook: A Critical Look at Research & Practice in Helping Professions.* (With Robert Alexander, Peter Breggin, Jeffrey Buck, David B. Cheek, Juanne Clarke, Frank Epling, Stanley Fevens, David Frey, John Friedberg, Glen Gabbard, D'Arcy Helmer, Lenore Jacobson, Mark Kamlet, Richard Mason, Michael Miller, Geoffrey Nelson, Carl Rogers, Robert Rosenthal, Jalal Shamsie, Thomas Szasz, Benjamin R. Tong, Stuart Twemlow, Kenneth Walker, J.B. Woodward). 456 Pp., Albuquerque, NM: Morgan Foundation. (1st edition: Toronto: IPI)

Morgan (2012). *Trauma Psychology in Context: International Vignettes and Applications from a Lifespan Clinical-Community Psychology Perspective.* Santa Cruz, CA: Morgan Foundation.

Morgan (2021) *Time Statues*. Santa Fe, NM: Winds of Change Press.

Morgan, R.F. & Toy, T.B. (1970). Learning by teaching: a student-to-student compensatory tutoring program in a rural school system & its relevance to the Educational Cooperative. *Psychological Record*, 20, 159-169.

Morgan, R.F. & Elkind, L. (1972) National Institute of Mental Health Children's Community Mental Health Center Grant for the John Hale Health Foundation, National Medical Association, Bayview-Hunters Point, San Francisco. Empowerment model: Coordinated by single-parent interns for their own children and for prevention intervention with community children.

Morgan, R.F. & Toy, T.B. (1974) "Learning by teaching: A student-to-student compensatory tutoring program and the educational cooperative." In J.G. Sherman (Ed.), *Personalized System of Instruction (PSI) Germinal Papers: Selected Keller Plan Readings*. Menlo Park, CA: W.A. Benjamin, Inc., 1974, 180-188.

Moulon, R. & Morgan, R.F. (1967) Sibling bondage: A clinical report on a parricide and his brother. *Bulletin of the Menninger Clinic*, 1967, 31, 229-235.

Neill, A.S. (1978) *Freedom-not license!* London: Pocket.

Neill, A.S. & Lamb, A. (1995) *Summerhill School: A new view of childhood*. New York: St. Martin's Griffin.

Reich, W. (1981) *Record of a friendship: The correspondence between Wilhelm Reich and A.S. Neill 1936-1957*. New York: Farrar, Strauss, Giroux.

Roach, M. (2021) *Fuzz: When Nature Breaks the Law*. New York: Norton.

Rogers, R. (2011) *Destiny's Landfall: A History of Guam*. Honolulu: University of Hawaii Press.

Roske, Allan. (1984). *Predicting Violence in a Maximum-Security Penitentiary: A Matter of Survival*. Ph.D., California School Professional Psychology, Fresno.

Rossi, E.L. & Cheek, D.B. (1994) *Mind-Body therapy: methods of ideodynamic healing in hypnosis*. N.Y.: Norton.

Segal, R. (2016). "The Case for a Central Patient Portal for Medical Records". *Huffington Post*, 31 August. https://www.huffingtonpost.com/entry/the-case- for-a-central-patient-portal- for-medical-records us 57c5e17de4b07addc40f87ba

Seneca (65BCE, 2004) *On the Shortness of Life: Life is Long Enough if You Know How to Use It*. New York: Penguin.

Shaked, Y., Michael, Y., Vered, R.Z., Bello, L., Rosenbluh, M., & Pe'er, A. (2018). Lifting the bandwidth limit of optical homodyne measurement with broadband parametric amplification. *Nature Communications*, 9 (1).

Sherman. J.G. (1974) Learning by teaching: A student-to-student compensatory tutoring program and the Educational Cooperative". In J.G. Sherman (Ed.), *Personalized System of Instruction (PSI) Germinal Papers: Selected Keller Plan Readings*. Menlo Park, CA: W.A. Benjamin, Inc., 1974, 180-188. Reprinted from the 1970 publication in *The Psychological Record*.

Shapiro, J. (1970*). Investigating the effectiveness of sensitivity training of nurses on the progress of their patients.* Unpublished PhD dissertation at the University of Waterloo, Ontario, Canada.

Simard, S. (2021) *Finding the Mother Tree: Discovering the Wisdom of the Forest.* New York: Knopf Doubleday.

Slattery, U. (2005). *Unfortunate baby names: Slattery's complete collection of the most notable ten thousand for dramatic or other usage.* N. Charleston, SC/ Grass Valley, CA: Morgan Foundation.

Toch, H. (1980) T*herapeutic communities in corrections*. New York: Praeger.

Toch, H. (1995) "Inmate involvement in prison governance." *Federal Probation*, 59, 34-39.

Toch, H. ((1997) *Corrections: A humanistic approach*. Albany, N.Y.: Harrrow & Heston.

Toch, H. (2017) *Violent Men: An Inquiry into the Psychology of Violence*. 25th Anniversary Edition. Washington, DC, American Psychological Association.

Von Uexkull, J. (1957). A stroll through the worlds of animals and men. In C.H. Schiller (editor) *Instinctive Behavior*. New York: International Universities. 5-80.

Wohlleben, P. (2018) *The Hidden Life of Trees: The Illustrated Edition*. Vancouver, Canada: Greystone.

Wohlleben, P. (2019) *The Secret Wisdom of Nature: Trees, Animals, and the Extraordinary Balance of All Living Things — Stories from Science and Observation (The Mysteries of Nature, 3)*. Vancouver, Canada: Greystone.

Woolf, N.H. & Silver, C. (2018) *Qualitative Analysis Using MAXQDA*. New York: Routledge.

Woolman, M. (1967) *The basal progressive choice reading program*. Atlanta: Institute for Educational Research.

Robert F. Morgan

Born in the lull between the two world wars, he now shares his lifespan perspectives on today's interesting times with us.

Robert F. Morgan, Ph.D. is a Life Member of the American Psychological Association. An NIMH Pre-Doctoral Fellow at Michigan State University, he continued with more than 60 years of post-doctoral practice and teaching experience.

A former speech collaborator and project consultant for organizations including Dr. Martin Luther King Jr., he was founding editor of the Cambridge University Press Journal of Tropical Psychology, and founder of the Division of Applied Gerontology in the International Association of Applied Psychology (IAAP). He has overseen 126 psychology doctoral dissertations in California, Singapore, and

Australia, along with a contemporary trauma psychology seminar at the University of New Mexico. He has published more than a hundred articles and 17 books on topics including life span psychology, trauma psychology in context, applied gerontology, international psychology, and even unfortunate baby names.

Only semi-retired, he avoids a lethargic status by continuing to think and write. He also hopes to avoid that opposite error exemplified by misleading voices of our era and, of course, Lincoln's prescient warning: *"It is better to be silent and thought a fool than to open one's mouth and remove all doubt."*

Well, his readers will continue to be the judge of that.

Optional Theme: *Peter and the Wolf instrumental* (New York Stadium Symphony Orchestra) **https://www.youtube.com/watch?v=Fmi5zHg4QSM&ab_channel=NewYorkStadium-SymphonyOrchestra-Top**

Other Books by Robert F. Morgan

Time Statues

Trauma Psychology in Context: International Vignettes and Applications

Opportunity's Shadow & the Bee Moth Effect: When Danger Transforms Community

Growing Younger: How to Measure & Change Body Age

The Iatrogenics Handbook: Research & Practice in Helping Professions

Training the Time Sense: Hypnotic & Conditioning Approaches

Unfortunate baby names: Slattery's complete collection with the most notable thousands for dramatic and other usage

Electroshock: the Case Against.

Directory of International Consultants in Psychology

Interventions in Applied Gerontology

Measurement of Human Aging in Applied Gerontology

Should the Insanity Defense be Abolished?

Conquest of Aging: Modern Measurement & Intervention

The Effective Verbal Adaptation (EVA) test: Parts A & B

The Educational Status of Children in a District without Public Schools: CRP 3221.

The Educational Status of Children during the First Year Following Four Years of Little or No Schooling: CRP 2498.

Uncas Slattery and the Muddy Chuckle

www.ingramcontent.com/pod-product-compliance
Lightning Source LLC
Chambersburg PA
CBHW041137110526
44590CB00027B/4052